SIERRA STORIES

SIERRA STORIES

TALES OF DREAMERS, SCHEMERS, BIGOTS, AND ROGUES

GARY NOY

FOREWORD BY MALCOLM MARGOLIN

Heyday, Berkeley, California
Sierra College Press, Rocklin, California

This Sierra College Press book was published by Heyday and Sierra College.

Library of Congress Cataloging-in-Publication Data

Noy, Gary, 1951-
  Sierra stories : tales of dreamers, schemers, bigots, and rogues / by Gary Noy.
    pages cm
  Includes bibliographical references.
  ISBN 978-1-59714-265-6 (softcover : alkaline paper)
  1. Sierra Nevada (Calif. and Nev.)--History--Anecdotes. 2. Sierra Nevada (Calif. and Nev.)--Biography--Anecdotes. 3. Sierra Nevada (Calif. and Nev.)--Social life and customs--Anecdotes. 4. Sierra Nevada (Calif. and Nev.)--History, Local--Anecdotes. I. Title.
  F868.S5N69 2013
  979.4'4--dc23
                          2013037067
Cover Art and Design: Ashley Ingram
Interior Design/Typesetting: J. Spittler/Jamison Design
Printing and Binding: Thomson-Shore, Dexter MI

Sierra Stories was published by Heyday and Sierra College. Orders, inquiries, and correspondence should be addressed to:

Heyday
P.O. Box 9145, Berkeley, CA 94709
(510) 549-3564, Fax (510) 549-1889
www.heydaybooks.com

10 9 8 7 6 5 4 3 2 1

FOR
MOM AND DAD

CONTENTS

FOREWORD

by Malcolm Margolin

Those of us who live in the San Francisco Bay Area *go* to work, we *go* to school, we *go* to the store, but we *escape* to the mountains. We escape the way a prisoner escapes from jail, a high school student plays hooky, a sailor heads out on shore leave. We run off with deep delight and near total abandon. We shed restrictions, obligations, and expectations; we leave the humdrum behind. In the Sierra we can be free, we can climb, hike, ski, swim, drink, or gamble. In the mountains we can play.

There are things we can do in the mountains that we can't do elsewhere, but perhaps more to the point, there are things that we can't do. We can't farm very well in the mountains; the soil and climate discourage that. The blessed absence of farming was keenly felt, especially in the Gold Rush era. What caused the world to rush in was not just the lure of instant wealth but an opportunity to escape the farm. In the mid-nineteenth century, the great majority of Americans lived on small family farms, enslaved by the endless demands of milk cows, chained to the remorselessness of the crop cycle, working from dawn to dusk, and sometimes into the night. Those who weren't farmers didn't have it much better, having to endure the tedium of factory work, the deadly routine of keeping shop, the degradation of civil service, and (although generally unspoken) the straitjacket of family.

I have often thought about the young men of the East Coast, setting out for the distant goldfields of California. There are tears in their eyes as they say farewell and receive the blessings of aged parents, as they clutch a photograph of loved ones to their chests, as they tenderly hide a locket of hair and a love note among their belongings. Those about to leave do everything they can to present themselves as dutiful sons, faithful husbands, and caring fathers setting off on the quest of the hero, the wealth quest, to bring back the gold that will free their families from toil and poverty. It is part of their image as providers, as loyal family members. I know that the tears are real—these were sad and emotional moments. But would you think badly of me if I were to suggest that beyond the tears was a part of them itching to get away from the importunities of a spouse, the criticism of parents and neighbors, the whining of children, and the never-ending lowing of the damn milk cow? That they were, at least in part, deliriously happy to leave the "business" of life to the polite, the timid, the obedient, and the prudent who would stay behind, have tea on Sundays, and go to church while the wild ones broke loose and headed for the hills?

And once the traveler found himself on the road, might we not imagine that another freedom appeared, addictive and intoxicating in its seductive power: freedom from truth? I know this goes against the dictum that "the truth shall set you free." I know I'm butting heads against the foundations of modern therapy and the scores of self-help ideologies that teach us to acknowledge our problems and tell us that the road to happiness is through a deep understanding of the truth of our being. But let me at least put forth the notion that for many, especially those with dull lives, the truth is nothing but a set of shackles. It's fantasy and imagination that set us free, and the young men (and sometimes the young women), out of earshot of those who knew them from birth, were able to take on other identities, embrace other fantasies, and fill themselves up with the power, the promise, and excitement of being not who they were but who they wanted to be.

Could anyone ask for a better breeding ground for stories? Here was a world free of laws—not only the laws of society but even the laws of logic. Who needs prudence when fantasy opens its arms and embraces us? What a cascade of bravado, enterprise, and folly. Take the time, for example, in 1850, when a disheveled vagabond stumbled into a Sierra mining camp and told of a lake ringed with gold nuggets. A witness later described the "perfect stampede" that ensued. "Since Peter the Hermit led his army of fanatics towards Palestine, no such incoherent crowd has been seen as that which rushed through the forest and trailless mountains in quest of this golden delusion." Everywhere, the "golden delusion," a.k.a. El Dorado, beckoned, and tens of thousands answered the call.

The Sierra Nevada, with its 14,000-foot granite peaks, crystalline lakes, conifer forests, and hidden valleys, became, and in some ways still is, the domain of dreams, attracting the heroic and the delusional, the best of humanity and the worst. Over the decades, characters have emerged so outlandish and outrageous that they have to be real. Could the human imagination have invented someone like Eliza Gilbert? Born in County Sligo, Ireland, in 1821, she changed her place of birth to Seville, shed a few years from her birth date, and took the name Lola Montez, bringing to Gold Country the provocative "Spider Dance," in which she impersonated a young woman repelling a legion of angry spiders under her petticoats. Or Otto Esche, who in 1860 imported fifteen two-humped Asian bactrian camels to transport goods to the mines. Or the artist Albert Bierstadt, whose paintings Mark Twain characterized as conveying "more the atmosphere of Kingdom-Come than of California." Or George Whittell, Jr., owner of the Thunderbird Lodge in Lake Tahoe, who at the end of his life withdrew from people, preferring the company of an elephant named Mingo, a lion named Bill, cheetahs, polar bears, and other wild animals.

In 1853, when the Irish-born singer Kate Hayes, billed by P. T. Barnum as "the Swan of Erin," toured California, a front row seat at the theater was auctioned off at $1,200. For so much less money—and, one suspects, greater comfort—this collection of Sierra stories offers us a front row seat too: the backdrop is the Sierra itself, and on the stage is a cast of characters that pays tribute to the restless, dynamic enterprise of our species and the art of good storytelling.

A word about the storyteller: Gary Noy is a scholar, a teacher, a mentor, and a thoroughly decent man. He taught history at Sierra College in Rocklin for more than twenty years, and he is a founder and director emeritus of the Sierra College Center for Sierra Nevada Studies. I'm happy to report that despite his education Gary can spin a good yarn, and indeed he keeps us well entertained. Read this book for the joy of the storytelling, but be aware of another current that runs through it. At the hands of someone else, the characters that spill out of these pages might be presented with mockery. If you are looking for mockery, looking for an easy sense of how superior we are to the fools on the page, you might look elsewhere. Something deeper is stirring here. Along with the fun, we feel in these stories a sense of the courage of people, a compassion for those whose hopes were dashed, a rage against the assault upon native people and the brutal suppression of the immigrants, in all a love and respect that Gary as a native son has for the place in which he has lived so deeply and to which he has devoted so much of his life.

Those of us who live in places like Berkeley escape to the Sierra. Gary was born and raised here; this is home. So stop listening to me, a stranger to these parts. Let us gather around the campfire and look toward the kind and intelligent soul who is so patiently awaiting his turn. Hey, Gary! Tell us some good stories!

PREFACE

Just a few miles from Beckwourth Pass in the northern Sierra Nevada is the tiny crossroads town of Vinton. Located in Plumas County and on the cusp of the massive Sierra Valley—thousands of acres of agricultural land skirted by forests—it isn't much to speak of. Vinton's most prominent feature is a combination post office/convenience store/gas station, and beyond that, there isn't much else. Unless you notice that just outside the hamlet lies an old masonwork Western Pacific Railway bridge spanning two lanes of blacktop. It is a portal to the Sierra Nevada, a symbolic doorway to the geography of dreams, a landscape of imagination.

Pass through the arch and you are ushered into 400 miles of undulating topography, a humpy-bumpy serpent scaled with lofty granite spires, rocky knobs, and dramatic monoliths. We see wildflower carpet, unhurried glaciers, snow-laden recesses, and stairstepped foamy river courses. The range is whiskered with conifers and oaks and scrub from its verdant foothills to its imposing alpine zone to its deserty apron on the Great Basin. We all know the scenery, we have seen it a thousand times. Close your eyes. Imagine Yosemite Valley. In your mind's eye, it is there. It is real. As celebrated photographer Ansel Adams once famously stated: "A large granite mountain cannot be denied."

But there is more to the Sierra Nevada than just the spectacular panorama. There is the fascination of the miniscule, the attraction of the rare, the unearthing of the unusual, and the type of sublime microcosm that led the illustrious naturalist John Muir to spend hours studying an ant crawling on a dead pine during his first summer in the Sierra.

And so it is with many of the remarkable stories of the people of this "Range of Light." There are countless tales of magnificent and tragic human endeavors in the Sierra—stories of measured optimism and overwhelming disappointment; renewal and reinvention; the chronicles of folks seeking a better life, and of those who were just stuck. These narratives enthrall us. These cultural memories both inspire and trouble us.

Among them are many accounts that are by now mostly forgotten—obscure accounts that bypassed the history books and became tangled in the shadows. These are the triumphs of simple living, of failures and futility, and of the comic and sometimes heartbreaking reality of life in the range. *Sierra Stories* focuses on some of these overlooked narratives and hopefully releases them from the dark, forgotten recesses of history.

While our attentions are understandably drawn to accounts of the epic terrain or the famous personalities, it is often the smaller, hidden moments that provide the unique color and distinctive texture that gives us a nuanced perspective of the Sierra experience. Just as an artist can enhance a monumental landscape painting with the deft application of a tiny dab of pigment, so can these little-known tales supply a richer, more inclusive portrait of the Sierra Nevada.

Traditional encyclopedias present the most familiar facts about a person, place, or concept, but, in the pages that follow, the emphasis is not general information but the uncommon details. Each quasi-encyclopedic entry is accompanied by a shorter feature called a "Sierra Spotlight" that highlights a tale of similar nature. For a few readers, these stories will be old friends, but for most these will be surprises, maybe even revelations.

My personal tale of the Sierra Nevada opens in my hometown of Grass Valley, the Nevada County foothill settlement where I was born in 1951. Grass Valley had been a major gold mining center since the earliest days of the Gold Rush, and it was still a mining town, but by the 1950s it had grown tired and careworn. The Grass Valley of my youth was threadbare and grimy, a workingman's town, but I was nevertheless enchanted. Around every corner waited towering mine buildings, rusting industrial equipment, and a pageant of wondrous curiosities. My best and most lasting memories are of playful diversions, mysterious locations, and spots of magnificent peculiarity. These settings have always fascinated me, and perhaps that is why I've been drawn to the untold stories of the Sierra ever since. One such intriguing locale was just down the street from where I grew up. It is here that our journey into the surprising Sierra Nevada will begin.

MISS CATHERINE HAYES

AS ZERLINA, IN FRA-DIAVOLO.

"Oh, holy Virgin! whom I adore,
Lorenzo's fate and mine watch o'er."

Act I. Sc. 1.

3/61

THE SWAN OF ERIN

The Enduring Legacy of Kate Hayes

There is a curious little street, basically an overgrown alley, dark, shadowy, and exotic, that leads up the hill toward the Empire Mine grounds in Grass Valley. It is called Kate Hayes Street. Kate Hayes is a well-known name with a remarkable story—an important entry in the Gold Rush chronicle.

Entertainment was considered as important as air in the goldfields of that era. Life was hard, and the brutal truth was that most participants in the quest for quick riches failed, and not just simply but spectacularly. They lost their life savings or staked bad claims or were swindled in town or worked endless hours knee deep in ice-cold mountain streams to secure just enough gold dust, just enough color, to buy that night's dinner. It was a difficult, frustrating world, and a few hours'

Playbill highlighting Kate Hayes as Zerlina in the Daniel Auber opera *Fra Diavolo*, c. 1850. Courtesy of the Folger Shakespeare Library, Washington, DC, ART File H417 no. 1 (size XS).

respite from the drudgery was welcome if not necessary to survival. Escapism is not a recent concept.

Catherine "Kate" Hayes was not after ore in the hills, but she was part of the Gold Rush just the same. She was born in Limerick, Ireland, in 1818, and her childhood was a sad story of desperation and dire poverty. But Kate was talented, and as a young woman her exquisite singing voice gained local and regional notice, even though her natural skill was untrained, unpolished. In 1839, she began formal voice training, and in 1842, she traveled to Paris, armed with letters of introduction from Antonio Sapio, her singing instructor and accompanist. Almost immediately, she found a teacher: the celebrated master Manuel García. After several years of operatic study under García, Kate Hayes debuted at the Marseille Opera in May of 1845. She was a sensation. A leading newspaper in Milan, *La Fama*, cooed that she had "a voice of delicious quality."

A few months later she performed at what was widely considered the preeminent European opera house—Milan's La Scala. The reviews were glowing. The emerging diva began to be known by the public as "The Hayes" or "La Hayez." Shortly thereafter, Giuseppe Verdi, the famous composer, became interested in her for one of his new operas. Her great success continued throughout Italy as well as in Vienna, and she soon became the era's most sought-after soprano for Gaetano Donizetti's *Lucia di Lammermoor*. After one Venetian performance of *Lucia*, a local critic reported that

> after the cavatina the enthusiasm was almost fanatical; the rondo finale created a hurricane of applause and bravos….
> At the end of the performance La Hayez was called before the curtain three times with the applause lasting a full ten min-utes….La Hayez could not desire a more splendid triumph.

As her fame spread, songs were composed especially for the new star, and a racehorse was even named Catherine Hayes in her honor.

In June 1849, Hayes received an invitation to sing at Buckingham Palace for Queen Victoria and five hundred guests. After an evening of Italian music, the queen requested an encore. Hayes sang the senti-mental Irish ballad "Kathleen Mavourneen," her signature tune. It was widely believed to be the first time a popular Irish song had ever been performed in the palace. In her diary that night, Queen Victoria wrote: "Miss Hayes [sang] very nicely & with much feeling & a good method."

In November 1849, Hayes returned to her native country of Ireland. Her homecoming as a worldwide cultural heroine resulted in sparkling notices for her performances in operas and concerts throughout the Emerald Isle. Typical was this review in Dublin's *Freeman's Journal*, from November 6, 1849:

> The reception for Mademoiselle Hayes was, beyond con-
> ception, enthusiastic. But on the last evening, the peals
> of applause that greeted each effort of our Irish soprano,
> were worthy of the theatre....Miss Hayes sang an air
> "Why do I weep for thee?" [and] a rapturous encore
> followed; but instead of repeating the song...[she per-
> formed] the sweet Irish ballad "Kathleen Mavourneen,"
> [and] the audience were at once stilled into silence...
> [by Hayes] rendering the sweet and heart-breaking music
> of this exquisite melody with a degree of pathos, feel-
> ing and taste, that kept the audience as if spellbound....

At a benefit concert a few days later, Hayes charmed the audience with her rendition of "The Return to Erin," a song composed for her by her accompanist Julius Benedict especially for the occasion. The lyrics included this lovely thought, which deeply touched the hearts of her Irish audience:

> So my fond heart with rapture is burning,
> Dear Erin, to see thee once more.
> When far, far away on the ocean,
> I have sighed for my dear native shore,
> And prayed, with the purest devotion,
> For the day I should see it once more.

In 1851, Hayes came to America, where she faced stiff competition from a wide variety of performers, most notably Jenny Lind. But there was something special, something transcendent, about Kate Hayes, and she eclipsed them all.

Hayes presented sold-out concerts throughout the Midwest, New England, and the Atlantic seaboard. She traveled south to forty-five different venues, including many in the major river towns along the Mississippi, among them New Orleans. She met and fascinated many political, civic, and business leaders along the way, including President Millard Fillmore. During this tour, Kate was also destined to meet her future lover and husband—Jenny Lind's former manager, William Bushnell.

Also in 1851, Hayes's travels took her to the California goldfields, where she became a particular favorite of the miners. With his unerring sense of how to make a buck, the great showman P. T. Barnum sponsored her tour. She was billed as "The Swan of Erin," or sometimes "The Hibernian Prima Donna."

The *Far West News* raved about her 1852 appearance at San Francisco's American Theater: "Long and loud were the cheers and applause, which greeted her entrée. She acknowledged again and again the enthusiastic testimonial, and again and again the audience cheered and applauded."

In a recent review of an excellent biography of Kate Hayes by Basil Walsh (Irish Academic Press, 2000), the *London Daily Express* wrote: "Hayes was the Madonna of her day; she was the 19th-century operatic equivalent of the world's most famous pop star." Although the two celebrities may have been similarly high-profile, they were certainly not similar in behavior. Throughout her career, Hayes enjoyed an unmarred reputation as a lady of supreme elegance and virtue. Reports of her public appearances frequently included observations such as these:

> The personal appearance of Miss Hayes is most attractive....
> We might regard her as the impersonation of the grace, and
> delicacy, and innocence of Irish modesty and Irish beauty.
>
> *Cork [Ireland] Examiner,* November 16, 1849

> [Kate Hayes is] the very personification of all that is
> graceful and elegant in woman; her eyes, dark blue,
> her teeth dazzling white, her finely formed lips slightly
> parted as though always anxious to speak some kind
> thing; her hair neither golden nor auburn, but with that
> changeful color which sparkles in the folds. Her face

highly expressive…of kindness—goodness of heart.

Saroni's Musical Times [New York], September 20, 1851

Miss Hayes is slightly above medium size, rather
delicately proportioned, with a quite pleasant but
not beautiful face. Her manner is easy and graceful, and her dress almost severely simple.

Cincinnati Gazette, April 7, 1852

Miss Hayes is not only a sweet singer, but her every ex-
pression and appearance denote her a sweet girl also. She
has a modest and most winning look, which with her fine
voice, and agreeable manners, and more than ordinary
personal beauty, make her an object of much interest.

Cleveland Plain Dealer, April 23, 1852

Miss Hayes is about thirty years of age. She is a graceful, queen-like person, of medium stature, with a fair
oval face. Her features are regular, hair bright auburn,
eyes blue, and her face wears an intellectual expres-
sion without much animation. She dresses with taste,
and her manner is perfectly easy and self-possessed;
her gesticulation appropriate and graceful.

Daily Alta California [San Francisco], December 1, 1852

It was this aura that the footloose young miners adored, for in those
wild settlements, in that wild time, Kate Hayes represented the girl next
door, that singular angel waiting back home.

Hayes's popularity cannot be overstated. On February 8, 1853, Kate
performed a concert in Sacramento for which seats were sold to the
highest bidders. A few days earlier, the Empire Fire Engine Company
had paid $1,150 at auction for the first seat to a performance in San
Francisco, and not to be outdone, Sacramento's Sutter Rifles held its
own auction for the best seat in the Sacramento house. The high bid
was $1,200 for a front row seat, and the ticket was presented to Captain
John Sutter—the same man who gave his name to Sutter's Mill, where
the discovery of gold instigated the California rush—who proudly took
his place on an ornate green sofa.

Through the spring of 1853, Hayes performed throughout Gold Country, visiting many mining camps and even trying her hand at gold panning. In a review of one of her last concerts, at the Alta Theater in Grass Valley on April 18, 1853, the *Nevada Journal* reported: "The voice of [Kate Hayes] broke forth in notes of most bewitching sweetness and harmony. The excitement of the audience increased to a furious extent, no doubt with proud ratification that they had heard for once in their lives, the voice that had awakened the admiration of the western world."

Mining communities throughout the foothills were captivated by the Swan of Erin, and before long the name "Kate Hayes" was cropping up all over the area: Kate Hayes Flat, Kate Hayes Hill, the Kate Hayes Mining Company, and of course that little street heading up to the Empire Mine.

Following her Gold Country tour, Hayes performed in South America, Hawaii, Australia, India, and Singapore, among other exotic locales, before returning to London in 1856. The following year she married William Bushnell, but after only seven months of marriage he died of what was then called consumption but was most likely tuberculosis. For a year following Bushnell's passing, Hayes did not perform and was rarely seen in public. When she eventually returned to the stage, she did so only briefly, and a few years later, in 1861, she died from a stroke at age forty-two. Citizens of her birthplace in Ireland were deeply saddened at the loss, and her hometown obituary was so long it had to be presented over two days in the *Limerick Chronicle*. The heartfelt reminiscence included these haunting words:

> [T]he profound sorrow with which the death of Catherine Hayes filled the public mind was universal. Her name was long associated with those sweet,...tenderest memories of youth and home and love, which none could portray with such vivid and thrilling effect as she did. Catherine Hayes dead! The sunlight itself looked sorrowful, and the earth seemed robed in mourning!

Several years ago, after I told this this tale of Kate Hayes to a Grass Valley audience, a woman approached me. She lived on Kate Hayes Street, but no one in her family had any idea of the history behind the street's name. She went on to say that once the family had taken up residence there, her mother, who had never liked opera music before, became nearly obsessed with one opera in particular: *Lucia di Lammermoor*, the favorite of Kate Hayes. This woman's childhood home, she recalled, was constantly filled with the thrilling sounds of recordings of the Donizetti classic. "Now, I would like to think that my mother loved this opera so much," she whispered to me, "because it was the spirit of Kate Hayes singing in her ears."

SIERRA SPOTLIGHT

Jenny Lind

In 1851, when Kate Hayes came to America, Jenny Lind, the "Swedish Nightingale," was already enjoying widespread adulation and was her greatest rival. The operatic soprano was so celebrated in Europe that the American impresario and flimflam artist P. T. Barnum signed Jenny to perform in one hundred concerts in the United States before he had even heard her sing one note. When a Nevada City theater named after Jenny Lind was demolished by a Deer Creek flood in March of 1852, the published reports that "Jenny Lind has disappeared" evoked deep sadness among those who thought the real Jenny had gone to meet her maker. A Gold Rush mining camp in Calaveras County was also named Jenny Lind in her honor.

Jenny Lind, the Swedish Nightingale, c. 1850. Photograph produced by Matthew Brady's Studio. From the Daguerreotype Collection, c. 1850, courtesy of the Library of Congress, Prints and Photographs Division, Washington, DC, LC-USZ62-110191.

852. Reflection in Donner Lake.   Mount Lincoln,

THREE MONTHS ALONE

The Ordeal of Moses Schallenberger

In the 1840s, the area that would become California might as well have been the far side of the moon for Americans. The distant Mexican province was mostly still a mystery, and what little was known was frequently inaccurate, yet all it took were just enough rumors about fertile soil and endless opportunity to give adventurous Easterners incentive to attempt the perilous trek across the continent's interior. But maneuvering wagons over the Sierra Nevada summits seemed impossible. In 1841, the Bidwell-Bartleson Company struck out from Missouri for California carrying their earthly possessions and precious hopes in a wagon train. After getting lost in the eastern Nevada desert, the party abandoned its wagons and crossed the Sierra Nevada on horseback

Mount Lincoln and Donner Peak reflected in Donner Lake. This was Moses Schallenberger's view for three months during the winter of 1844–1845. Photograph by Lawrence and Houseworth, c. 1865. From the Lawrence and Houseworth Collection, courtesy of the Society of California Pioneers, Image #642 (SCP).

near present-day Sonora Pass. In 1843, the Chiles-Walker Party managed to get their wagons as far as the Owens Valley, at which point
they headed south on horseback and crossed the southeastern Sierra
Nevada at what would become known as Walker Pass.

Moses Schallenberger was a member of the Stephens-Townsend-
Murphy wagon company, the first to successfully cross the Sierra Nevada
in wagons. The fifty-member group left Iowa in May 1844, led by Elisha
Stephens (sometimes spelled Stevens), a former mountain man and
beaver trapper. The largest family in the company—a total of twenty-
three men, women, and children—was headed by Martin Murphy, Jr.
Among the smaller families heading west in search of new opportunity
and a fresh start was Dr. John Townsend, his wife, Elizabeth, and her
eighteen-year-old brother, Moses Schallenberger. Dr. Townsend would
become the first licensed physician in California.

By September, when the company reached the Humboldt Sink, the
leaders were uncertain as to which direction to travel. Caleb Greenwood,
known as the "Old Man," acted as the party's guide and engaged in sign
language conversation with an elderly Paiute Indian who claimed to know
the best route to California. The Paiute was none other than the chief of
the tribe, a man who had earlier traveled with explorer and statesman
John C. Frémont to California. Unable to understand the Paiute man's
name, however, the party bestowed upon him the title "Chief Truckee,"
probably a misinterpretation of a Paiute phrase meaning "very well." In
his published account of the trip, Moses tells what happened next:

> From [Chief Truckee] it was learned that fifty or sixty miles
> to the west there was a river that flowed easterly from the
> mountains, and that along this stream there were large
> trees and good grass….Although there was still a doubt
> in the minds of some as to whether this was the proper
> route to take, none held back when the time came to
> start. In fact, there was no time for further discussion.

Snow was beginning to fall and quick decisions had to be made. By
mid-October, the Stephens-Townsend-Murphy Party had reached today's Truckee Meadows; it took another week to traverse the twenty
miles westward to the confluence of Truckee Creek (today's Donner

Creek) and the Truckee River. It was November and the snow was nearly a foot deep.

The company split. A six-member horseback party would explore the Truckee River while the wagons would follow the creek, which seemed a more favorable route. The horseback troop, with four men and two women, crossed the Sierra Nevada at Lake Tahoe on November 16, 1844. Although Frémont had spied the lake from a distance several years earlier, this party is considered the first non-native group to set foot on the shore of Lake Tahoe. From there they continued west and, after much peril and adversity, finally reached Sutter's Fort on December 10, 1844.

The wagon company did not do as well. Moses Schallenberger described the promising first days:

> [We] commenced the ever-to-be remembered journey
> up the Truckee to the summit of the Sierra. At first it was
> not discouraging….Then the hills began to grow nearer
> together, and the country was so rough and broken that
> they frequently had to travel in the bed of the stream.
> The river was so crooked that one day they crossed it ten
> times in traveling a mile….The whole party was greatly
> fatigued by the incessant labor. But they dared not rest.

And then it got worse. A foot of snow fell and more seemed probable. Reaching the present location of the town of Truckee, the company surveyed an apparently impregnable obstacle: the steep, imposing granite escarpment hundreds of feet tall to the west of a lake, which the party called Truckee Lake, later renamed Donner Lake. Moses recalled the site:

> The party with the wagons proceeds up a tributary…
> when they came to the lake since known as Donner
> Lake. They now had one mountain between them and
> California, but this seemed an impassable barrier. Several days were spent in attempts to find a pass.

With the oxen weakened and injured, some in the party abandoned any attempt to cross this forbidding wall with their wagons, but a few made the leap of faith and proceeded onward.

All the wagons were unloaded and the contents carried up the hill. Then the wagons were doubled and the
empty wagons were hauled up. When about half way
up the mountain they came to a vertical rock about ten
feet high. It seemed now that everything would have to
be abandoned except what the men could carry on their
backs. After the tedious search they found a rift in the
rock, just wide enough to allow one ox to pass at a time.
Removing the yokes from the cattle, they managed to
get them one by one through the chasm to the top of the
rock….Then the men lifted the wagons, while the cattle
pulled at the chains, and by this ingenious device the
vehicles were all, one by one, got across the barrier.

Three men were sent back to the lake to guard the remaining wagons until the spring thaw. Among them was the gawky teenager Moses
Schallenberger. The trio constructed a rough cabin, twelve by fourteen
feet and roofed with hides and pine boughs. This crude structure would
also be used several years later by the Breen Family of the ill-fated Donner Party.

And then the snowfall came in force. Soon, the snowpack had
reached the roofline, and the three men resolved to escape on snow-
shoes over the summit. They struggled to the top, but Moses developed
severe leg cramps and could not continue. After bidding farewell to
his compatriots, he limped back to the cabin to wait out his fate. The
eighteen-year-old spent the next three months isolated in that crude
shelter. He had some supplies stored away, but he planned on trapping
coyotes and foxes for sustenance. Moses hated coyote ("I ate this meat,
but it was horrible") but savored the taste of fox ("The meat, though
entirely devoid of fat, was delicious").

Mostly he wrote of being scared and lonely:

My life was more miserable than I can describe. The daily
struggle for life and the uncertainty under which I labored
were very wearing. I was always worried and anxious, not
about myself alone, but in regard to the fate of those who
had gone forward. I would lie awake nights and think of
those things….For some reason I would talk aloud to myself.

The wagon party struggled. Only twenty miles west of the summit, they established a survival camp for the exhausted oxen and forty-two company members. On December 6, 1844, a rescue party of seventeen departed the camp for Sutter's Fort. They did not return until February 1845 because they had been coerced into participating in a short-lived revolutionary action for political control of Mexican-ruled California later called the Micheltorena War.

When the rescuers finally arrived on February 24, the wagon company was surviving on boiled hides. No one had died, but many were desperate, and disaster was surely averted. Immediately taking their leave, the party quickly pushed below the snow line and on to the safety and warmth of Sutter's Fort.

One member of the rescue party, Dennis Martin, continued over the snow toward Truckee/Donner Lake and Moses Schallenberger. Laboring through snowdrifts, Martin reached the frozen lake and found Moses, still alive but emaciated. He was rescued and happily rejoined his family and friends. By June 1845, the snow finally melted and some members of the original party returned to Truckee/Donner Lake to retrieve the wagons they had left behind. When they arrived, the wagons were still there, but all their possessions—except, perhaps surprisingly, a few guns—had disappeared.

And what of Moses Schallenberger? He settled into farming life in San Jose and lived to the ripe old age of eighty-three. A forested granite spur on the southern shore of Donner Lake was christened Schallenberger Ridge in his honor.

SIERRA SPOTLIGHT

The Stephens-Townsend-Murphy Party

While his story may have been the most dramatic, Moses Schallenberger is not the only member of the Stephens-Townsend-Murphy party whose name lives on.

Company captain Elisha Stephens initially settled in San Jose before moving to the Bakersfield area. Using the alternative spelling of his last name, Stevens Creek runs through Santa Clara County, and several other namesakes—including a county park, a reservoir, a trail, a city district, and an elementary school—are located throughout the state.

Dr. John Townsend, brother-in-law to Moses Schallenberger, was not only the first licensed physician in California but also an early alcalde (similar to a mayor) of San Francisco. Townsend Street in that city was designated in his honor.

The foothill town of Murphys is named after patriarch Martin Murphy's sons.

Caleb Greenwood, the company's guide, eventually returned to Idaho to lead more wagon trains to California, albeit using shorter, less difficult routes than the one used by the Stephens-Townsend-Murphy Company. The Old Greenwood resort development in Truckee bears his name.

Two children were born during the 1844 passage, and as the men above gave their names to the land, the land gave their names to these babies. Mrs. James Miller gave birth at Independence Rock, Wyoming—to a little girl christened Ellen Independence Miller—and Mrs. Martin Murphy, Jr., had a daughter at the survival camp on the South Fork of the Yuba River. She named the baby Elizabeth Yuba Murphy.

The only known photograph of Elisha Stephens, leader of the Stephens-Townsend-Murphy Party, c. 1860. Courtesy of the Collections of the Sunnyvale Historical Society and Museum, Sunnyvale, California.

A BROAD,
HARD-BEATEN
ROAD

Melissa Coray and the Mormon Battalion

In 1848, Melissa Coray was only twenty years old but had already experienced a lifetime of adventures. Two years earlier, when Melissa Burton had married twenty-three-year-old William Coray in Mount Pisgah, Iowa, little did the newlyweds know that less than thirty days later William would be called to join one of the most distinctive military expeditions in American history—the march of the Mormon Battalion—and Melissa would go with him. It's their arduous journey back to Utah that is the main focus of this entry.

The Mormon Battalion was the only religion-based unit in United States military history. The battalion was a volunteer force organized by the Church of Jesus Christ of Latter-day Saints in 1846 in exchange

The Mormon Battalion Reunion of 1896. Melissa Coray is seated fourth from the left, under the cannon barrel. Courtesy of the Research Center, Utah State Historical Society, Salt Lake City, 973.62 no. 21558.

for government protection during a period of intense religious perse-cution. In February 1846, the Mormons had fled westward across the Mississippi River, away from violent mobs destroying their settlement in Nauvoo, Illinois. Brigham Young, president of the Latter-day Saints, sought federal assistance for the Mormon refugees, and sent an emis-sary, Elder Jesse Little, to Washington, DC, to plead their case. Little arrived in the nation's capital on May 21, 1846, only eight days after the United States had declared war on Mexico. Elder Little met with important political figures, including President James K. Polk, and in June of that year, a skeptical Polk agreed to provide aid if the Mormons volunteered their service in the fight against Mexico. He requested five hundred Mormons to join the American cause.

Brigham Young gave his public approval, stating that what the president wanted was "to do good and secure our confidence." He reassured his people that "the outfit of this five hundred men costs us nothing, and their pay will be sufficient to take their families over the mountains [to California.]...The thing is from above for our own good."

In Iowa, the five hundred enlistees were recruited over a period of three weeks. Accompanying the men would be thirty-three women—twenty of whom served as laundresses—and fifty-one children. One of the recruits was Sergeant William Coray, and one of the laundresses was his new bride, Melissa.

In July 1846, the Mormon Battalion, under now Brigadier General Stephen Kearny, began its two-thousand-mile trek across the Great Plains to California. They arrived in San Diego in January 1847 and, until their discharge in July of that year, the Mormon Battalion primar-ily performed occupation duties in Southern California. There were no combat casualties, but twenty-two men died from diseases or other non-combat-related causes during their enlistment.

Following their service, members of the Mormon Battalion spread throughout California. Despite Brigham Young's admonition to resist the allure of gold, some worked for John Sutter and James Marshall at Sutter's Mill in Coloma at the time of the gold discovery in Janu-ary 1848. Mormon Battalion veteran Henry Bigler recorded the date of Marshall's historic discovery in his diary—January 24, 1848, which thereafter became the accepted historical date of the event.

The majority of the group's members, however, wished to rejoin their families in the now burgeoning Mormon capital next to the Great Salt Lake in the mountain desert of what would later become Utah.

In May 1848, several of the battalion veterans reconnoitered a new wagon route over the Sierra Nevada to the east, hoping to find a more hospitable road than the California Trail, which required the wagon train to cross the Truckee River twenty-seven times. After a three-day journey from Sacramento and just barely into the mountains past Placerville, the surveyors found themselves nearly buried in snow. One of their donkeys, one member recalled, was up to his eyes in snow and would only budge when they tugged on his long ears, which occasionally popped above the snow line. Having reached a ridgetop that gave them a view east of nothing but snow-strangled passes, they naturally decided to postpone the trip a few weeks until the snow melted.

In June, the homesick veterans tried again. Three scouts were sent to determine a possible path while the others gathered near Sly's Park, a settlement near today's Pollock Pines. On July 10, with the scouts having not yet returned, the party began its difficult, trackless journey east. This company would be the only major wagon train to deliberately travel west to east during the height of the Gold Rush. It consisted of forty-five men; seventeen wagons; two small Russian cannons purchased from John Sutter; 450 horses, mules, and cattle; and one woman, Melissa Coray. The road they were breaking is known today as the Mormon Emigrant Trail, a hundred-mile path that connects Placerville and western Nevada.

An early resolution to avoid the deep, rocky canyons and thick forests and instead follow the ridges did not eliminate the need for backbreaking labor. Clearing the wagon road required cutting gnarly brush, prying massive boulders and tossing countless rocks from the path, and making slow, steady, sweaty headway. A growing, gnawing concern was the condition of the three missing scouts.

Work continued as apprehension intensified. Wooden cart axles snapped, metal wagon rims and other needed replacement parts were hand-forged on the spot, unattended animal stock wandered away, and the resilient undergrowth was unrelenting. Through it all, the lone woman, Melissa Coray, continually cooked and cleaned for the dozens of hardworking men.

Responding to growing unease about the fate of the scouts, Henry Bigler and three others forged ahead ten miles to seek the absent pathfinders. The search party glimpsed some Indians at a distance, and several men remarked that the natives were wearing clothes very similar to those of their missing friends. Bigler's squad retreated, but not before they came upon a fresh grave in a stand of trees. Fearful of an Indian attack, they rushed to rejoin their comrades, who now, considering the ominous discovery a warning, posted guards through the night.

Two days later, on July 19, the party slowly approached the unmarked gravesite. The grave was opened, and stacked inside they found the nude, blood-spattered bodies of the three missing scouts. One scout's face had been crushed with an axe and shot in the eye. Bloody arrows and rocks were scattered nearby. That evening the party was understandably skittish. Melissa Coray considered it one of the worst days of her life. In the dark of night, a mysterious noise spooked the animals, and the group decided to discharge a cannon as a warning to any intruders. The echoing boom ricocheted rapidly around the granite canyons, frightening the horses and mules. The next morning, one-third of the animal stock was missing.

That afternoon, a deeper grave was prepared, the three scouts were reburied, and the site was piled high with stones to keep wild animals from disturbing the remains. Someone carved the names of the fallen on the trunk of a balsam fir tree as a memorial, and today the carved portion of the tree is on display in Coloma. The party gave the gruesome burial ground an appropriate name: Tragedy Spring.

The Mormons had traveled thirty-nine grueling miles in fifteen days, but the most dangerous and difficult portion lay ahead. Fifteen of the men set out to fashion a road to the top of a nearby mountain ridge. It was the end of July and they found nearly twenty feet of snow.

The task at hand was to construct a road over glistening granite laced with volcanic rock and basalt. Boulders as tall as ten feet blocked the path. Melting snow made the way sloppy and slippery. The work-force set bonfires next to the colossal granite boulders and then split the superheated rocks into smaller chunks. Wagons were particularly vulnerable to damage, and every day witnessed several of them over-turned, cracking their tongues and spokes. Finally, on July 24, the group crossed the summit at West Pass, but not before four more wag-ons broke down. The elevation at the crest is 9,500 feet, the highest point reached by any overland wagon trail in the American West.

On July 28, the party blazed a road through a slender notch now known as Carson Pass, named after John C. Frémont's famous scout, Christopher "Kit" Carson, who had scrambled over the summit a few years earlier. The group rested at a site it called Summit Camp, and nearby was a tree upon which Carson had carved his name and the date of his crossing: February 14, 1844.

Only a few feet east of the pass, a sheer escarpment waited. Steep, almost perpendicular rock walls had to be mastered. One frightfully abrupt palisade was dubbed the Devil's Ladder. At this cliff, the men physically wrestled the wagons to keep them from tipping, while with block and tackle they delicately lowered the wagons to a safer level.

Finally, the Mormons descended into a large alpine valley, which they gratefully named Hope Valley; for the first time in a long while they believed a safe arrival in Salt Lake City was possible. To celebrate, Melissa prepared a pot pie consisting of trout, four "mountain chick-ens" (as noted by Henry Bigler in his diary), and two ducks. By early August, the weary company reached the Carson Valley and connected with a spur of the California Trail.

It had taken the Mormon Battalion veterans about a month to forge the Mormon Emigrant Trail, but the effort was not soon forgotten, and they were far from the last to travel the winding road, in either direction. On their way east, the party encountered many hopeful goldseekers head-ing westward toward the Mother Lode, and the trail the Mormon party blazed became a major thoroughfare to the land of glittering dreams. An estimated 50,000 wagons and 200,000 emigrants used the road during the Gold Rush. In 1854 alone, the official wagon register for this stretch records 800 wagons; 30,015 head of cattle; 1,903 horses and mules; and

8,550 sheep on the now broad, hard-beaten road. Within a decade, this 107-mile route from Nevada to Placerville sprouted about forty commercial establishments of rest and accommodation—one roughly every three miles.

The veterans of the Mormon Battalion arrived in Salt Lake City in late September 1848—three months after their journey began. Only a few short weeks after reaching their destination, William Coray, weakened by exposure and adversity on the journey, died at age twenty-five. Melissa remarried and spent the rest of her life in Utah, dying at age seventy-five in 1903. A few years before her death, Melissa Coray made a brief return to the Sierra Nevada and revisited some of the venues of their memorable passage.

In 1994, the United States Board of Geographic Names christened a 9,763-foot peak overlooking Kirkwood Meadows and Carson Pass in honor of all the pioneer women who sacrificed and served during the nineteenth-century migration to and from California. The peak is named Melissa Coray Peak. The commemorative plaque was unveiled by eight-year-old Melissa Richmond, the fourth-great-granddaughter of Melissa Coray.

SIERRA SPOTLIGHT

George Stoneman

While the Mormon Battalion was a unique unit, it was still part of the United States Army and had non-Mormon officers. One of them was George Stoneman, who served as quartermaster of the battalion. His name may sound familiar, particularly for those who have visited Yosemite Valley.

George Stoneman was a career military officer who rose to the rank of Major General. A West Point graduate, his academy roommate was Confederate icon Thomas "Stonewall" Jackson. Stoneman commanded a crack Union cavalry force during the Civil War and spearheaded surveying parties seeking railroad lines through the Sierra Nevada. Following his military career, Stoneman entered politics and was the fifteenth governor of California, from 1883 to 1887. George Stoneman is commemorated by Camp Stoneman, a military base near the Carquinez Strait in the San Francisco Bay Area, and by Stoneman Meadow and Stoneman Bridge, near Camp Curry in Yosemite Valley. From 1887 to 1896, an imposing hotel stood in the valley at the foot of Half Dome. It was named the Stoneman House Hotel, in George's honor.

Major General George Stoneman, quartermaster of the Mormon Battalion and a Civil War cavalry officer, c. 1865. Photograph from the Brady National Photographic Art Gallery, from the series "Selected Civil War Photographs, 1861–1865," courtesy of the Library of Congress, Prints and Photographs Division, Washington, DC, LC-DIG-cwpb-05212.

MORE
BEAUTIFUL THAN
THE ORIGINAL

Albert Bierstadt

For the grand landscape painters of the nineteenth century, the Sierra Nevada was a seductive subject, its virgin soil and granite ripe for interpretation. Their missions and visions changed how the landscape was comprehended and, in return, the land altered the trajectory of not just American art but American politics as well. With a dab of color here, an imaginative addition there, these prominent artists defined our relationship with the Sierra, our perception of nature, and the future of the range.

The four best-known and most influential painters of the Range of Light were Albert Bierstadt, Thomas Hill, William Keith, and Thomas Moran. They shared a common artistic heartbeat—Yosemite Valley—

Albert Bierstadt, painter of monumental Sierra Nevada landscapes, c. 1875. From the California History Room Picture Collection: Albert Bierstadt, no. 1991-0928 [carte de visite], courtesy of the California State Library, Sacramento.

and through their work, the region became more than just an exquisite wonder; it became a symbol of preservation, of natural longing and national destiny.

Albert Bierstadt was the first of the quartet to be professionally associated with the gorgeous granite gulch of Yosemite Valley. Born in 1830 in Germany, Bierstadt was two years old when his parents moved the family to Massachusetts. Demonstrating an early interest in art, young Bierstadt dazzled his parents with fanciful crayon sketches. In his early twenties, Albert returned to Germany to study with masters of the Düsseldorf School of Painting. After returning to New Bedford, Massachusetts, and establishing a studio, in 1859 Bierstadt accompanied General Frederick Lander on a United States government survey expedition to the Rocky Mountains and the Pacific Coast. He turned his rough sketches of the excursion into many finished paintings and thus started his long love affair with the American West panorama.

In 1863, Bierstadt and some fellow landscape artists visited Yosemite for the first time. Accompanied by journalist Fitzhugh Ludlow, Bierstadt was instantly smitten with the valley's grandeur. Ludlow described their initial glimpse of the landscape from Inspiration Point as "an unspeakable suffusion of glory created from the phoenix-pile of the dying sun." Bierstadt used this and other memories of Yosemite to produce monumentally grand paintings of this extraordinary mountain cathedral. Adopting an artist-explorer persona, Bierstadt painted what were commonly called "Great Pictures"—that is, large-scale paintings that toured the country to attract critical attention and wealthy buyers. Due to the work of the Hudson Valley School and its leader Frederick Church, landscape paintings had gained immense popularity. As Church popularized Niagara Falls, Yosemite Valley became the creative axis for Bierstadt.

In 1865, Bierstadt displayed his initial Yosemite painting, the five-by-eight-foot *Looking Down the Yosemite Valley, California*. Introduced to the public in New York City, the painting was exhibited throughout the country and cemented Bierstadt's reputation as the premier interpreter of Western vistas. The gigantic canvas also gained the notice of collectors. The piece was particularly attractive to the American expansionists, who viewed all things American as bigger, better, and more beautiful than what had come before; it was a land dominated by grandiose expectations and Manifest Destiny in an age of global transformation rightly led, the ardent nationalists argued, by unbridled confidence in American ideals. Bierstadt's work reflected those notions. On his canvases, Yosemite Valley was a temple to a divine plan for the country. His work fed the dream and fetched high prices.

Bierstadt played the part of the prosperous artistic impresario as well. He was acutely aware of the value of marketing, and in his case the product was not only his paintings but himself. During the 1860s and early 1870s, Bierstadt happily assumed the pose of sophisticated artiste. With a commanding presence and his beautiful wife, Rosalie, by his side, Bierstadt became a celebrity in the United States and abroad. His works, and Bierstadt himself, were exhibited throughout continental Europe. He counted the rich and the powerful—even royalty—among his closest acquaintances. And they provided Bierstadt with lucrative commissions on both sides of the Atlantic.

Respected not only for his artistic ability but also for his entrepreneurial acumen, Bierstadt was spirited, uncompromising, perceptive, and self-made—all attributes widely venerated in the last half of nineteenth-century America. Bierstadt was the most highly esteemed and richest painter of his time, although he remained at the pinnacle for only a decade, as changing tastes and critical disapproval tempered the intensity of his fame.

Railroad financier and treasurer of the New York Stock Exchange LeGrand Lockwood admired *Looking Down the Yosemite Valley, California*…he just thought it was too small. Lockwood commissioned Bierstadt's second, even more enormous Yosemite Valley work, *The Domes of the Yosemite*. Completed in 1867 and measuring a mammoth nine and a half feet tall and fifteen feet wide, it was Bierstadt's biggest canvas and his most controversial painting. While some argued that the painting was his artistic acme, many others were brutal. Typical was acerbic *New York Tribune* art critic Clarence Cook, who dismissed *The Domes of the Yosemite* as maladroit and vulgar and evidencing "little accurate knowledge of nature." Other critics were contemptuous of Bierstadt generally, scorning his excessive romanticism; his overenthusiastic use

of dramatic elements such as golden light, fog, clouds, and mist to emo-
tionally manipulate the viewer; and his occasional willingness to alter the
details of a landscape to suit his needs. Some found that his use of color
did not reflect natural reality: Bierstadt's flora was always lushly green,
even when it was not actually so. When *The Domes of the Yosemite* was
unveiled, critical derision kept audiences comparatively sparse. Mark
Twain initially refused to examine the painting, believing the prevailing
wisdom of the cognoscenti that a visit was not worth the time. When
Twain finally saw the massive composition, he declared, in typical
Twain fashion, that the painting was "considerably more beautiful than
the original....[It] is altogether too gorgeous..., more the atmosphere
of Kingdom-Come than of California."

Contemporaneous to the painting's controversy and criticism,
Congress passed the Yosemite Grant Act of 1864, which declared that
Yosemite Valley and the Mariposa Grove of Big Trees would be admini-
stered and protected by the State of California. The combination of the
grant and the publicity of Bierstadt's *Domes of the Yosemite* led to increased
attention on the valley as a whole and ultimately fostered "a violent out-
break of Yosemite views, good, bad and indifferent," as San Franciscan
Benjamin Parke Avery noted in an 1868 *Overland Monthly* article. Among
them, Bierstadt's works were the most popular due to the dissemination
and sale of affordable chromolithographic prints of his works.

Despite the mixed reaction to his Yosemite pieces, Bierstadt popularized the valley as both a stunning realm of the picturesque and an icon
of national pride. His reputation and popularity waned as monumental
canvases went out of style, and art historians remarked that his later
work did not have the intensity, freshness, or craft of his earlier efforts.
Bierstadt's paintings may not have been culturally chic in his later years,
but he remained well-liked in the general public throughout his life.

Bierstadt lived until age seventy-two, and some have estimated that
he produced nearly four thousand paintings during his lifetime. Most
would agree that he achieved his greatest success in his thirties...
unless you count his current popularity. In 2008, the United States
Postal Service issued a stamp featuring Bierstadt's 1864 work *Valley
of the Yosemite*—calling the piece an "American Treasure"—and many
of his landscapes are found in prominent museums worldwide. His

prints are still widely available, and one could argue Bierstadt is more fashionable now than in his own day.

SIERRA SPOTLIGHT

William Keith

In the nineteenth century, William Keith was one of the grandest and most significant painters of the majestic Sierra Nevada landscapes. He was also a great friend of John Muir's. Born in Scotland in 1838, Keith immigrated to the United States at the age of twelve, worked as a magazine illustrator at age twenty, studied painting on the side, and, in 1868,was commissioned by the Northern Pacific Railroad to paint landscapes of locations along the company's route.

On an 1872 visit to Yosemite Valley, Keith first met John Muir, who became a close friend for the next forty years. Muir encouraged Keith's landscape painting and urged him to depict the natural world with clinical precision and accuracy. Keith's artistic sensibility allowed him, however, to at times deviate from geologic reality, enriching a landscape by adding a stream here or some other nonexistent feature there. Keith felt that subjective enhancements gave his landscapes additional emotional value, but Muir objected and the pair argued. In fact, they bickered about everything, albeit privately; to the wider world, there was no doubt how much Muir valued his friend. Muir extolled Keith as an important and influential painter of poems, exalting nature in pigment just as Muir would in prose.

William Keith was a crucial participant in an inner circle of Muir friends who met frequently in San Francisco to discuss the establishment of a Yosemite National Park. In 1892, under Muir's leadership, members of this assembly—Keith among them—formed the Sierra Club.

William Keith, painter of epic Sierra scenes and a close friend of John Muir, c. 1900. From the California Faces Collection, courtesy of The Bancroft Library, University of California, Berkeley; Keith, William–POR 31.

FEARFUL
SYMMETRY

Native Americans in Early California

The seasons are spectacular in the Sierra Nevada. Winter drapes the range in a luxurious ermine cloak, spring adorns it with a rainbow of vibrant wildflowers, summer displays wind-roughened lakes, and fall enlivens the crisp air with cascading leaves. Throughout the year, the Sierra is bathed in its distinctive light, a watercolor wash of reds and oranges and yellows that saturates and slithers, casting elongated shadows in a variety of hues. In this splendid environment, it is hard to imagine anything sinister.

When European culture arrived in Alta California in 1769 in the form of the Catholic Church, intent on building a string of Franciscan missions along the Pacific coastline, it is estimated that the Indian population of the region numbered about three hundred thousand.

A family portrait of Yosemite Valley natives. From a stereograph by Gustav Fager-steen, c. 1875. Courtesy of the California History Room Picture Collection: Stereo Collection: Indians: fagersteen NN, no. Stereo–2530, courtesy of the California State Library, Sacramento.

By 1860, the figure had dwindled to about thirty thousand, a result of disease, cultural and physical dislocation, and outright murder. Tribes on the coast were particularly devastated by illness and by forced subjugation to the Catholic missions under Father Junípero Serra, whereas natives in the interior valleys fared somewhat better in their resistance to encroachment. Indians living in the Central Valley, foothills, and Sierra Nevada areas were spared significant European settlement until the arrival of John Sutter at his inland kingdom of New Helvetia—today's Sacramento—in 1839.

In 1847, an Indian guide escorted James Marshall to the Maidu village of Collumah, on the American River. Marshall, who had been hired by John Sutter to construct and manage a sawmill in the Sierra foothills, decided the location was perfect. The area, soon to be known far and wide as Coloma, offered readily available building materials, easy access to the Sacramento Valley, and an abundant labor force of Maidu Indians. Ultimately, more than half of Marshall's Coloma workforce were natives.

January 24, 1848, is the day James Marshall is credited with discovering gold in the tailrace of the mill under construction, a find that instantly set off the world-renowned California Gold Rush. While some have argued that the actual find was made by one of Marshall's Maidu employees, no one disputes that the event at Sutter's Mill changed the direction of Californian, American, and world history. It also forever altered the lives of the Sierra Nevada natives. Within a few years, more than half of California's Indians were dead—victims of disease but also oppression and violence.

Thousands upon thousands of goldseekers swept across the landscape like an avalanche, and the official government policy toward the natives became "extermination." Arguments for following precedent and removing the Indians to reservations were drowned by sentiments like those expressed by Governor Peter Burnett, in his first annual message to the newly created state legislature in 1851: "That a war of extermination will continue to be waged between the two races until the Indian race becomes extinct must be expected; while we cannot anticipate this result with but painful regret, the inevitable destiny of the [Indian] race is beyond the power and wisdom of man to avert."

Public policy supported the barbarous practice. Local governments provided bounties for Indian heads or scalps. In 1855, Shasta City offered five dollars for every severed Indian head deposited at city hall. Witnesses described mule trains arriving in town carrying eight to twelve Indian heads. In 1859, near Marysville, bounties "for every scalp or some other satisfactory evidence" of an Indian death were paid by public subscription. Honey Lake, in the northern Sierra, paid twenty-five cents for Indian scalps.

At the state level, volunteer militia members submitted claims to the California State Treasury for reimbursement of their expenses in "suppression of Indian hostilities" and extermination. In 1851 and 1852, the legislature appropriated funds for claims totaling more than $1 million. Eventually, the federal government reimbursed the state government for these ghastly expenditures.

It was also open season on the legal rights of Indians. In April 1850, the new California State Legislature passed "An Act for the Government and Protection of Indians." This humane-sounding law was anything but protective. Any Indians were subject to arrest "on the complaint of any resident" if they could not financially support themselves or if they were "strolling about [loitering]" or "leading an immoral or profligate course of life." If the government determined that an Indian was a "vagrant," he or she could be bought within twenty-four hours from a county or municipal agency at public auction and forced to work for a term not to exceed four months. The 1850 law also provided that a convicted Indian could be bailed out "by any white person" willing to pay the fine and that "the Indian shall be compelled to work for the person so bailing, until he has discharged or cancelled the fine assessed against him." Many reports indicate that when an Indian's service was nearing an end, it was not unusual for the overseer to ply him with liquor, have him arrested for public drunkenness, repurchase the Indian at auction, and renew control of the victim. The act stated that "in no case shall a white man be convicted of any offence upon the testimony of an Indian."

A final provision of the act established a system of Indian "apprenticeship," under which any white person desiring the labor of an Indian child could appear before a justice of the peace and make a petition for the right of custody. The action required the supposed consent of the child's "parents or friends." If the justice agreed, a certificate was issued authorizing "the care, custody, control, and earnings of such minor, until he or she obtain the age of majority." Under the law, whites could obtain the services of any number of Indian males under the age of eighteen and females under the age of fifteen. The only obligation of the master was to treat, feed, and clothe the underaged wards properly. Failure to meet that condition resulted in reassignment of the child to another master and a ten-dollar fine.

In 1860, the apprenticeship provision was revised to allow children to be placed in a master's custody without parental consent. It was also altered to permit "articles of indenture" that authorized the white overseer to have control over the Indian charge for a set period of time: males under fourteen could be detained until the age of twenty-five and males obtained between the ages of fourteen and twenty could be controlled until the age of thirty. Females could be retained to the age of twenty-five.

It is believed that three thousand Indian children were sold into slavery at between $50 and $200 apiece under California's sanctioned "apprentice system." Kidnapping was not unusual. In 1855, the Alta California reported, "It has been the custom of certain disreputable persons to steal away young Indian boys and girls, and carry them to white folks for whatever they could get. In order to do this, they are obliged to kill the parents." In 1856, Thomas Henley, Superintendent of California Indian Affairs, reported to George Manypenny, Federal Commissioner of Indian Affairs: "It is proper to say that [kidnapping] has been carried on to an extraordinary degree. I have undoubted evidence that hundreds of Indians have been stolen and carried into the settlements and sold; in some instances, entire tribes were taken en masse."

Indian girls were often sold or kidnapped and forced into sexual slavery. Kidnappers prized physical beauty, and one Nisenan mother stated that she would deliberately dirty her children's faces to keep them from being kidnapped. In his 1858 memoir, Isaac Cox described the purchase of an eight-year-old Indian girl by a white settler named Kentuck. The girl, wrote Cox, was "either for his seraglio [harem], to be educated the queen of his heart, or the handmaid of its gentle emanations."

Native women were also frequently kidnapped and forced into prostitution. In El Dorado County in 1853, two Indians attempting to free their captive wives were shot, one fatally. In 1856, the *San Francisco Bulletin* reported that in one mountain reservation "some of the agents, and nearly all of the employees [were] daily and nightly...kidnapping the younger portion of the females, for the vilest purposes....[These] wives and daughters [were] prostituted before the very eyes of their husbands and fathers, by these civilized monsters."

The Act for the Government and Protection of Indians ultimately placed local natives into various forms of slavery or near-slavery and remained in effect until 1863, when it was repealed as a result of President Abraham Lincoln's Emancipation Proclamation. It is uncertain exactly how many Indians were affected by the original 1850 legislation, but historian Robert Heizer estimates that as many as ten thousand Indian boys and girls may have been indentured, kidnapped, or sold between 1850 and 1863.

The fates of most of the children are unknown. Consider the case of Isabella, an eight-year-old Indian girl living with the Gomez family in San Francisco in 1856. Isabella had been with the family since 1852, but it is unclear how she joined the family or what her role was within it. It is certain that on Monday, December 8, 1856, at five o'clock in the afternoon, a stranger presented himself at the Gomez residence and announced that Isabella belonged to him. She was turned over to the mysterious visitor and they disappeared. Soon afterward, another man arrived claiming that Isabella was his property and demanded the Gomez family produce the missing girl. They could not. As reported in the *San Francisco Herald*, family matriarch Charlotte Sophie Gomez testified in court that she had "no knowledge of the person who took the child from her house, nor does she know where she is, or has been, since taken away."

SIERRA SPOTLIGHT

Judith Lowry

Native American authors, painters, photographers, linguists, and histo-rians are at the forefront of the resurgence, or perhaps resurfacing, of attention to Sierra Nevada Indian heritage. A prime example is Judith Lowry, a painter of unusual power and storytelling skill. Born in 1948, Lowry is of Pit River and Mountain Maidu ancestry and focuses her art on the traditions and realities of California Indian life. In 2004, she pro-duced the monumental six-panel *Weh-Pom and the Star Sisters*, depicting Weh-Pom (Coyote) traveling to the stars to seduce five celestial sisters. The sisters wear flicker feather headbands, shell necklaces, and tule skirts and, having rejected Weh-Pom's unwanted advances, they cele-brate by dancing with stars and comets. In 2009, *Weh-Pom and the Star Sisters* was purchased by the Smithsonian Institution National Museum of the American Indian. Judith Lowry has exhibited at the Crocker Art Museum in Sacramento; the Wheelwright Museum of the American Indian in Santa Fe, New Mexico; the C. N. Gorman Museum in Davis, California; the Heard Museum in Phoenix, Arizona; and the George Gustav Heye Center in New York City.

Maidu artist Judith Lowry, c. 1990. Photograph by Dugan Aguilar. Gelatin silver print, 8 x 10 in. In the collection of the Oakland Museum of California, gift of the photographer, no. 2000.16.3. Used by permission of Dugan Aguilar.

SOLID GOLD FISHHOOKS
The Gold Lake Excitement of 1850

In the shadow of the Sierra Buttes in Nevada County is a splendid realm of many crystalline, trout-laden lakes and regiments of spiky green conifers. Now called Lakes Basin Recreation Area, it is also the place where miners' dreams ran wild during the height of the Gold Rush. It was a time when men hoping to strike it rich would believe just about anything. An advertisement in the Richmond, Indiana, *Palladium* of February 7, 1849, offered "California Gold Grease" to those heading for the western hills: "The operator is to grease himself well, lay down on top of a hill, and then roll to the bottom. The gold, and 'nothing else,' will stick to him. Price $10 per box." This clever entrepreneur was not selling ointment but something more important: a fantasy.

In 1850, a mysterious vagabond named Thomas Stoddard stumbled into a mining camp at Frenchmen's Bar along the Yuba River, a

Miners at work at the Young American Mine, near the Sardine Lakes in the Gold Lake region, Sierra County, c. 1880. From the Hendel Collection, General Views, California History Room, no. 2008-0521, courtesy of the California State Library, Sacramento.

few miles from the little town of Washington. A sympathetic resident named W. C. Stokes took him in, and over dinner, Stoddard recounted his intricate life story, highlighting his experiences as a wounded British war veteran, a hopeful immigrant, a newspaper editor, a schoolmaster, and a frustrated goldseeker. Stoddard's tale was not unusual at that time and in that area—virtually everyone had come from somewhere else and had a story to tell—and Stokes paid little attention to the details. Stoddard's narrative did include one unusual account, however. He told Stokes of a fabulous place he had discovered high in the mountains near Yuba Pass—a lake ringed with gold nuggets. Stokes considered the story just another tall tale with exaggeration and ornamentation, and when Stoddard moved on he dismissed the entire encounter as a trifle. At least, that is, until Stoddard reemerged some weeks later with a sack full of gold.

Stoddard described to everyone who would listen how he and several companions had returned to the beautiful mountain lake wreathed in remarkably rich deposits of gold nuggets resting on the shore and in the lake moss. Gold was *everywhere,* glimmering in the sun. Stoddard and his fellow explorers were busy gathering the shiny specimens when they were attacked by Indians. Stoddard's leg was severely lacerated, but he was the single member of his group to survive, escaping only just barely and with merely a small sample of the gold they had discovered. Stoddard's sack contained more than just a few gold nuggets, and the specimens were assayed and found to be very pure. With this evidence in hand, Stoddard's story was no longer doubted, especially as there had been a number of splendid strikes throughout the region.

Stoddard quickly organized an expedition to return to the golden lake. The party swelled in anticipation of the gold chunks soon to be lining their pockets. At this point, Stokes approached Stoddard to reacquaint himself, but Stoddard was belligerent in his refusal to acknowledge his former host. Caught off guard by this unexpected turn, Stokes began to feel uneasy about the endeavor and cautioned the feverish participants to be wary of Stoddard's claims. His warning would be of no avail.

Fortified with optimism, Stoddard's eager mob set out to claim their golden windfall. Soon, however, their fortunes seemed less certain. Stoddard acted disoriented, perplexed. He became increasingly frustrated and unsure about his destination, meandering aimlessly, visiting other, smaller lakes, none of which he recognized. After many days, the party arrived at a large body of water, although much larger than the golden lake Stoddard had described. The befuddled Stoddard pointed and, with hesitation, declared, "This looks like the one." The zealous goldseekers thoroughly prospected the lake but found nothing. The expedition named the location "Gold Lake" in anger, a title that endures today.

Some argued that Stoddard had simply made a mistake, but most were indignant, concluding that Stoddard was a charlatan, the architect of an elaborate deception. As a final challenge, the exasperated party of a few dozen men charged Stoddard to find the golden lake within twenty-four hours *or else*. If he did not? Thomas Stoddard would hang.

The next morning, Stoddard had disappeared. Clearly, he had lied, and there was no golden lake. The crestfallen expedition scattered, with many exploring the nearby streams and river forks in search of some small compensation for their efforts.

Then suddenly, after weeks of frustration, some of the miners found gold. Soon after, strike after strike was made in the area. Alonzo Delano, a merchant who would later gain fame as a popular humorist, was part of the "Gold Lake Excitement" and recorded some of the "practical and beneficial results" of the event:

> The country was more perfectly explored, some rich diggings were found, and, as usual, a few among the many were benefited. A new field for enterprize was opened, and within a month, roads were made and traversed by wagons, trading posts were established, and a new mining country was opened, which really proved in the main to be rich, and had it not been for the gold-lake fever, it might have remained many months undiscovered and unoccupied.

At the same time, many miles away, rumors spread that the magical lake had indeed been found. A preposterous spectacle followed. The failure of the Stoddard expedition notwithstanding, thousands left nearby Nevada City and Marysville and headed up to Gold Lake. News editors more interested in selling papers than setting the record straight asserted that "reliable" and "respected" sources had confirmed the lake's existence. Other accounts told of local Indians using the treasure to craft solid gold fishhooks and furniture. The exodus from Marysville in particular was a mad dash, and a complete one. As hundreds of miners surged to the lake, businesses closed and Marysville became a virtual ghost town overnight.

In November 1884, Henry Wells wrote an article for the *Overland Monthly* revisiting the entire affair. Wells described the "perfect stampede" to the region as a "side show" that had been given "the dignity of the main circus":

> All the floating population of the mines took the fever, and many, also, who owned good claims abandoned them to go where one day's work was worth a thousand....Hundreds had but an indistinct idea of what they were in search of; all they knew was that somewhere in the mountains was a place where gold could be picked up in chunks, and they proposed to get there in time to pick up a few for themselves.

As Wells concluded, "Since Peter the Hermit led his army of fanatics towards Palestine, no such incoherent crowd has been seen as that which rushed through the forest and trailless mountains in quest of this golden delusion." But delusion was enough for many.

Thomas Stoddard himself soon resurfaced and declared that his original story was true, all true, and upon that claim he sought financing for a new journey. A number of respected citizens invested heavily in Stoddard's latest scheme and sought to publicly discredit any Stoddard critic. An 1858 newspaper account recalls that Stoddard was roundly absolved of the original fiasco, the finger instead pointing absurdly at W. C. Stokes for supposedly engineering the entire travesty for his own benefit.

In truth, the golden lake, as Stoddard had described it, was never found. The fervor eventually subsided, but the rumor has never completely vanished, and probably never will as long as people dare to dream big dreams.

SIERRA SPOTLIGHT

E Clampus Vitus

Many Gold Country communities make a case for being the original home of E Clampus Vitus, a fraternal organization dating back to the Gold Rush known for its splendid iconoclasm, but Mokelumne Hill in Calaveras County may have the best claim. In 1851, J. H. Zumwalt established the first formal, successful chapter of the group—ECV Lodge No. 1001—in the tiny mining camp. E Clampus Vitus, or the "Clampers," began as the anti-fraternal organization, making fun of the more august clubs such as the Masons and Oddfellows. Just as these lofty organizations had their arcane rituals and histories, so did the Clampers. Even the group's slogan is a takeoff on the much more serious Latin inscriptions of the more austere fraternities. The Clampers' motto is "Credo Quia Absurdum," or "I believe because it is absurd."

Mokelumne Hill, Calaveras County, the original headquarters of E Clampus Vitus. Photograph by Jay, c. 1900. From the California History Room Picture Collection: Calaveras County: Mokelumne Hill, no. 2008-2037, courtesy of the California State Library, Sacramento.

Lola Montes

THE SPIDER DANCER

Lola Montez

Gold miners, far from home, lonely and often discouraged, desperately needed distraction. One entertainment queen of the Sierra Nevada provided glamour, pleasure, and scandal in the rough-hewn days of mid-nineteenth-century California. She was the Spider Dancer, Lola Montez.

Montez, the beautiful and spirited woman who danced her way to fame in 1840s Europe, claimed she was born in Seville in 1823. Actually, she was born Eliza (or Elizabeth) Gilbert in Grange, County Sligo, Ireland, in 1821. When Eliza was young, her father, a British army officer, was transferred to India, and fearing that she was growing up a "wild Indian girl," her parents returned her to England and a more tranquil and controlled childhood.

In the early 1840s, Eliza burst on the public scene, having reinvented herself, and her history. According to her fanciful autobiography, she

Lola Montez, the Countess of Landsfeld, c. 1855. From the California Faces Collection, courtesy of The Bancroft Library, University of California, Berkeley; Montez, Lola–POR 4.

was of Spanish nobility, born with the stately name of Maria Dolores de Porris y Montez—called Dolores, or Lola, for short—and she was feisty to a fault. One contemporary, Miska Hauser, a violinist in Lola's theatrical troupe, described her thusly:

> Frivolous, naughty as a little child; can charm with
> a wink....She has a very excitable nature and for the
> slightest reason her whole body will tremble and her
> eyes flash lightning. For this reason one has to treat
> her carefully because she is the most courageous and
> foolhardy woman who ever walked the earth.

In her early twenties, Montez became notorious virtually overnight for her strange and provocative Spider Dance—a version of the Italian tarantella that cast her as a terrified young woman repelling a legion of angry spiders wreaking havoc under her petticoats. The *San Francisco Whig* of June 3, 1853, described the unforgettable dance:

> [After a wildly spinning entrance,] she unwittingly gets
> into one of those huge nests of spiders, found during
> the spring time in meadows, with a long radius of lead-
> ing spires and fibres, stretching away into an infinity of
> space. She commences to dance and the cobwebs entangle
> her ankles. The myriad spiders, young and old and half
> grown begin to colonize....It is Lola versus the spiders,...
> [and] she succeeds in getting the imaginary intruders
> away—apparently stamps daylight out of the last ten thou-
> sand, and does it with so much naivete that we feel sort
> of satisfaction at the triumph. The picture winds up with
> Lola's victory, and she glides from the stage overwhelmed
> with applause, and smashed spiders, and radiant with
> parti-colored skirts, smiles, graces, cobwebs and glory.

Her performance was a sensation, her private life outrageous and titillating. And it did not stay private for long. Montez married twice, took innumerable lovers (including the composer Franz Liszt and novelist Alexandre Dumas), and eventually became the mistress of Ludwig I, King of Bavaria, for two years. Love-struck Ludwig bestowed on Lola the title of Countess of Landsfeld and granted her real estate, expensive personal property, and undue influence in court, to the dismay of many. Georg von Maurer, an influential member of Ludwig's Council of State and a distinguished legal historian and jurist, expressed the widely held opinion, which was transmitted to the king by his principal minister, Karl von Abel: "[N]ational pride is deeply offended because Bavaria believes itself governed by a foreigner, whom the public regards as a branded woman, and any number of opposing facts could not shake this belief."

For many in Bavaria, the countess became a symbol of decadence and political corruption. George Henry Francis, a British correspondent for *Fraser's Magazine*, reported that Lola—whom Francis called "the fair despot"—had earned a pervasive public image as a capricious and rude schemer who "is passionately fond of homage…[and] merciless in her man-killing tendencies." In 1848, the chaotic Year of Revolution in Europe, anger and disgust over royal prerogatives in general and Montez's clout in particular reached the boiling point. Melchior von Diepenbrock, the Cardinal of Breslau, urged Ludwig to jettison his countess before it was too late:

> [She is] a poisonous tree [that] grows above you whose
> deadly perfume numbs you, robs your eyes of vision, intoxi-
> cates your senses and wholly beguiles you so that you see
> not the chasm before you, the open chasm that threatens to
> swallow up your honor, your reputation, the happiness of
> your family, of your land, of your life, as well as the salva-
> tion of your soul.…King Ludwig, awake from your dream!

Too late. *L'affaire Lola* would lead to Ludwig's abdication and years of social and political turmoil in Bavaria. Montez fled, but her reputation was a constant traveling companion.

In 1852, Lola Montez began a tour of America. In San Francisco, her Spider Dance was a spectacle. Audiences flocked to her curious performances, but it was not always artistry they appreciated; it was the opportunity to observe the scandalous celebrity in the flesh.

Once the initial commotion subsided, the increasingly sparse crowds realized Montez's act was mediocre at best. One rival offered a comic parody of her dance, and the once popular performer became a figure of fun, an object of ridicule. Audiences and critics began to publicly disparage and rudely heckle her during performances.

Incensed, Montez and her latest husband, a journalist named Patrick Purdy Hull, boarded a steamship for Sacramento. Hoping to escape harassment in the riverside boomtown, the couple was instead met with even more derision. Inevitably, the high-strung Montez reacted angrily and dramatically, as recalled by Miska Hauser:

> Lola made a gesture and the music ceased. Advancing daringly to the very edge of the stage, with pride in her bearing and fire in her eyes, she said, 'Ladies and Gentlemen, Lola Montez has too much respect for the people of California not to perceive that this stupid laughter comes from a few silly puppies.' Renewed laughter....She wished to go on, but the uproar had reached its culmination point; decayed apples and eggs shot through the air and the bombardment lasted so long that...with strategic backward movement [she] withdrew herself from the firing line.

Hauser leaped on stage to calm the audience with a violin solo, a tactic that was successful in that "the hall was turned from a madhouse into a theater." And then

> ...suddenly the persevering Spaniard [Montez] again appeared and in spite of the accelerated and wavering musical accompaniment she danced the spider dance to the end.... [With the performance concluded and the theater cleared, she departed but] when, Lola...reached the Hotel New Orleans, she was honored there with a serenade of awful cat-cries, broken pots and old kettles[;] flutes and drums added strength to this ear-splitting symphony. The fearless one appeared on the balcony and with a lamp and a shrill voice screamed at them: 'You cowards, low blackguards, cringing dogs and lazy fellows! I would not despise a dirty dog so much as I do you!'

She later clashed with the theater manager and challenged him to a duel. When his response was hearty laughter, Montez simply quit and left town immediately. Seething, she traveled northward to the mining community of Marysville, where her tour ended abruptly due to poor ticket sales and continued widespread mockery. Embarrassed, Lola Montez decided to leave the public arena, if only temporarily, and enjoy a respite from the madding crowd. Together with her husband she traveled to the flourishing gold mining town of Grass Valley, where she purchased a refuge, a modest home on Mill Street, the town's main thoroughfare. Today, a reconstruction called Lola's Cottage marks the location.

Even far from the big city, however, Montez was weighed down by the baggage of her outrageous reputation and she was spurned by Grass Valley's high society. She offered elegant entertainments and European-style salons for those who would dare to accept her hospitality, but few did.

Within days of her arrival, reports and rumors had surfaced of her history of appalling behavior. Some of the stories were true, some were not. It was accurately reported, for instance, that Montez had horsewhipped the local newspaper editor for publishing his derogatory comments about her. Less credible witnesses swore that Lola had shockingly and publicly performed her seductive dance for an objecting preacher. Even though most of the stories were false, Montez's actual behavior was more than enough to keep the gossips fascinated. Her backyard menagerie of a grizzly bear and several monkeys kept the locals intrigued, and her occasional loud arguments with her husband were public events. At one point, she banished Hull after he shot and wounded her pet bear. But generally, she puttered around the cottage, mostly tending to her garden and minding her own business.

Less well known—as is often the case with notorious figures—were her quiet acts of altruism. Montez financially assisted the town's needy and injured miners and nursed sick children. She even held a Christmas party for the little girls in town. But, as usual, the public craved scandal and these good works went largely unknown and unrecorded in the annals of history.

As Montez shrunk further from the spotlight, she was increasingly lonely and relished the visits of neighborhood children, many of whom probably passed by in hopes of seeing her exotic animals. One day, a new child paid a call. She was six-year-old Charlotte Crabtree, called Lotta by family and friends, and she lived just down the street.

From all accounts, Lotta adored Lola, and vice versa. Montez affectionately allowed the flame-haired waif to play with her costumes and dance with abandon to music from her ornate German music box. Although Lotta already attended a local dance class, Montez, marveling at the little girl's natural stage presence, devoted many afternoons to teaching Lotta extra songs and dances, eventually inviting her *protégé* to perform at her parties. Legend has it that the talented youngster gave her first public performance at the nearby mining camp of Rough and Ready. Reports claimed that the miners applauded enthusiastically when little Lotta danced on an anvil in W. H. Fippin's smithy while the blacksmith tapped out accompaniment with his hammer. Delighted by the response, Montez prophetically remarked that history would remember Lola Montez as notorious but would call Lotta Crabtree famous. And she was right. Within months, the now seven-year-old Lotta would leave Grass Valley and embark on an illustrious career, skyrocketing to fame as a beloved entertainer and, for many years, America's highest paid actress.

Following Lotta's departure, Montez grew bored, and in 1855, she left Grass Valley and embarked on a theatrical tour of Australia. It was an immediate flop. From there, she briefly returned to Grass Valley to sell the only home she ever owned. She left the mining camp, never to return.

Grasping for one last moment in the limelight, Lola Montez booked not a stage performance but a lecture tour. It too was a failure. Desperate and lonely, her finances dwindling rapidly, her health began to suffer, and the once famous Lola Montez receded into insignificance. Her later life was a constant battle with poverty and illness, and she eventually died miserable and penniless in 1861. She was only thirty-nine years old. A handful of newspapers ran obituaries, but her passing was mostly ignored.

SIERRA SPOTLIGHT

Adah Isaacs Menken

Gold Rush communities hosted many entertainers besides just the ultra-famous like the Spider Dancer, the Swan of Erin, and the Swedish Nightingale. Perhaps one of the most interesting was Adah Isaacs Menken, a featured performer in the popular melodrama *Mazeppa*. An accomplished equestrienne, Menken's primary contribution to the play was to be strapped to a horse that ran furiously on an inclined treadmill for fifteen minutes. Because Menken's character was a male, she was allowed the rare opportunity to crop her hair and—most impor-

tantly in the eyes of the mostly male audience—to wear flesh-colored tights, a bit of titillation that, in an era of strict Victorian standards, was positively scandalous. She received $500 per performance, the equivalent of *two years* of average annual income for a family of four.

Adah Isaacs Menken, the provocative Gold Rush–era entertainer. Original photograph from the George H. Johnson Photograph Gallery, c. 1855. From the Charles. B. Turrill Collection, courtesy of the Society of California Pioneers, San Francisco, C008741.

THE ETERNAL CHILD

Lotta Crabtree

She was known by many names—the Eternal Child, the Nation's Darling, the Fairy Star of the Gold Rush—but to residents of the Sierra Nevada, she was simply "our Lotta."

Charlotte Mignon Crabtree was born in New York City in 1847 to bookseller John Crabtree and his ambitious wife, Mary Ann. In 1851, seeking a new start in San Francisco, John Crabtree headed west alone, sending for Mary Ann and little redheaded Lotta in 1852. Upon their arrival in the City by the Bay, however, John Crabtree was nowhere to be found. Although they believed he was somewhere off in the goldfields, Mary Ann and Lotta were not exactly sure where. While they waited for news, they moved in with friends, some of whom were connected to the city's theatrical community. Lotta showed some interest in and aptitude for performance, so Mary Ann enrolled the little tyke in dance classes.

Lotta Crabtree in 1876. From the Jesse Brown Scrapbooks, vol. 10, 1996.003, vol. 10:42b–fALB, courtesy of The Bancroft Library, University of California, Berkeley.

In 1853, word finally reached Mary Ann that John was in Grass Valley, where he ran a boarding house, having struck out as a miner. When Mary Ann and Lotta arrived in the mining town later that year, Mary Ann discovered that their neighbor two doors down was Lola Montez, the infamous performer and Countess of Landsfeld. Mary Ann and Lotta introduced themselves, and Montez was enchanted by the bubbly little girl. The pair became fast friends, and the felicitous intersection of these two sparkling personalities would change the course both of their lives and of entertainment history. After a fashion, Montez mentored Lotta, teaching her a few performing tricks and giving her exposure in Grass Valley and beyond.

In 1854, the Crabtrees left Grass Valley and moved about forty miles north to an isolated mining camp deeper in the Sierra named Rabbit Creek (today's LaPorte in Plumas County). John once again tried unsuccessfully to strike pay dirt, and Mary Ann established another boarding house. By this point, Mary Ann was convinced that her child was especially gifted and provided additional singing and dancing lessons for Lotta. Within a year, Lotta Crabtree made her first professional appearance at Mart Taylor's local tavern.

A failed miner, Mart Taylor ran a saloon and an adjoining log theater, where he produced shows for miners and provided dancing and music lessons for the handful of local children, including Lotta. Taylor, Lotta later recalled, had arrived in Gold Rush California "with all kinds of air castles packed up in his carpet-bag. They toppled over as soon as he set them up, and he fell back upon music for a living." Taylor taught Lotta an assortment of jigs and reels, and Lotta came to be very fond of Taylor. In turn he found Lotta to be a delight and promised to showcase her in his theater.

In 1855, another tiny-tot entertainer arrived in Rabbit Creek. She was Sue Robinson, an already established child star, managed by Dr. David "Yankee" Robinson (no relation), a well-known goldfield impresario. Dr. Robinson attempted to book little Sue at Taylor's theater, but, determining that Taylor charged too much for the use of such rustic accommodations, he decided Sue Robinson would perform in another dance hall across the main street. Stung, Taylor retaliated by scheduling Lotta's professional debut the same night of Sue Robinson's appearance.

For the big show, Mary Ann Crabtree prepared a costume that was certain to delight the mostly Irish miner population of Rabbit Creek: a petite long-tailed green coat, green knee britches, and a tall green hat. Taylor, a part-time cobbler, fashioned a set of brogans and whittled a miniature shillelagh for the diminutive entertainer.

That night, eight-year-old Lotta Crabtree set foot on stage for the first time as a professional. In 1928, historian Constance Rourke described the scene:

> Since [Lotta] knew every one in the audience she was not shy. Casting aside the shillelagh, the absurd midget danced an Irish jig and reel. She always had a way of laughing when she danced, hard enough to achieve by design when every breath counts, but natural for her. She seemed tireless, a tiny bubbling fountain of fun and quick life. On the rough stage with candles for footlights in the midst of smoke and shadows she danced again and again....Then she appeared in a white dress with a round neck and puffed sleeves, and sang a plaintive, innocent ballad, looking like a pretty, little red-haired doll.

By the end of Lotta's performance, patrons had deserted Sue Robinson's show across the road and spilled into Taylor's theater to see "our Lotta." The audience showered the stage with quarters, half-dollars, Mexican pesos, a smattering of gold nuggets, and one five-eagle piece, an octagonal fifty-dollar gold slug. Mary Ann and Lotta quickly gathered the proceeds, and when the tally was made, little Lotta had earned more money in one night than her father had in four years of mining.

And so a star was born. It was the beginning of a spectacular career that would take Lotta Crabtree from the wooden plank stage of Rabbit Creek to the grand theaters of North America and Europe.

In 1856, when Lotta was still only nine years old, the family returned to San Francisco and used it as a headquarters for tours throughout California's Central Valley and the Sierra Nevada. Lotta was a darling of

San Francisco's music and variety halls, and by 1859, she was usually advertised as "Miss Lotta, the San Francisco Favorite" or "La Petite Lotta, the Celebrated Danseuse and Vocalist" and even the intriguing "Miss Lotta, the Unapproachable."

The reviews were sparkling. Starved for entertainment, not to mention female companionship, the denizens of California's mining towns were especially fond of young actresses and other female entertainers. These girls reminded the men of home and of genteel pleasures not often found in the rude camps. And Lotta, who grew up but always looked younger than her actual age, was a particular favorite.

Mary Ann Crabtree was an imperious stage mother but also a shrewd businesswoman. Not trusting paper money, Mary Ann insisted that Lotta be paid in coin or gold nuggets. Mary Ann did not have confidence in banks, so she deposited all of the girl's earnings into a big leather suitcase. When more space was necessary, the proceeds were carefully hidden in a steamer trunk. Once the steamer trunk was bursting, the money was invested in real estate and bonds. The family quickly grew wealthy. By now, John Crabtree was out of the picture. After allegedly stealing from Lotta's stage earnings, he was banished to England, where he lived on a small allowance provided by his estranged wife and daughter.

Lotta Crabtree toured the region for years, often in a string of grueling one-night stands, and she developed a passionate following. Part of her appeal was that her act remained remarkably consistent throughout the years, so the audience always knew what to expect; she sang uptempo tunes and ballads, danced energetically, made slightly naughty asides, and portrayed a wide assortment of *dramatis personae*, ranging from energetic Irish boys to sturdy Yankee sailors to comical Cockneys to delicate, sentimental belles. Her primary stage presence, however, was always that of a young girl, even as she reached middle age.

When not performing on variety stages or in music halls, Lotta acted in "legitimate" theater in California as well as on the East Coast and in the Midwest. She was very popular in plays written especially for her, including an adaptation of Charles Dickens's *The Old Curiosity Shop*, in which Lotta played both Little Nell and the Marchioness. A theater critic gushed that Lotta's performance was

> ...a performance *sui generis*. It is the quaintest, oddest conception in the world, and though it may be heresy to say so, her breakdown is the funniest thing ever done in comic dancing....Lotta's face as she sits down to the kitchen table, eyeing the dreadful mutton-bone, haunts me. No words can describe the fantastic tricks of this actress.

In a play titled *The Little Detective*, Lotta portrayed six different characters, and it was once reported that she sprinkled cayenne pepper into her red hair to make it sparkle on stage. A review from the *New York Times* had this to say about her stage persona: "The face of a beautiful doll and the ways of a playful kitten...no one could wriggle more suggestively than Lotta."

Lotta's reputation grew and grew. Poems, songs, waltzes, nocturnes, and polkas were dedicated to her. Play after play was written especially for her. Lotta never married, fearing that the audience would not accept her as the "eternal child" if she got hitched.

The money continued to flow in; during the 1880s she was arguably the nation's highest-paid actress, earning as much as $5,000 per week. Meanwhile, Mary Ann Crabtree continued to manage her daughter's career, handling financial affairs, booking plays, and organizing Lotta's touring company, a permanent acting troupe she traveled with starting in 1870, rather than using local stock companies. This was a highly unusual practice at the time, but such was the draw and power of Lotta Crabtree.

Mother and daughter sought continental cachet with a whirlwind tour of Europe in 1873. Lotta did not perform but rather burnished her image with Parisian French lessons, painting instruction, and piano study. Returning to America the next year, Lotta then swept through the country, charming the common people and the powerful. In New Orleans, Russian Grand Duke Alexis presented her with bracelets and a necklace festooned with diamonds and turquoise, and gave a lavish dinner in her honor aboard a Russian Imperial warship. Lotta was so much in demand as a dinner companion that each naval officer was only allowed ten minutes by her side.

In 1875, Lotta commissioned the elaborate, thirty-five-foot-tall "Lotta's Fountain" at the intersection of Market, Geary, and Kearny Streets in downtown San Francisco as a lasting mark of respect to the city's fans as well as in remembrance of the horse troughs that had provided relief to the exhausted and thirsty animals that she had seen in the city as a child. In the immediate aftermath of the 1906 San Francisco earthquake and fire, the fountain became an important gathering spot for survivors, and to this day San Franciscans continue the tradition of congregating there on the anniversary of the disaster.

Lotta Crabtree retired from the theater in 1892, at forty-five years old. She and her mother settled in New Jersey and purchased a cottage at Lake Hopatcong, where Lotta rode horses and pursued a newfound passion for oil painting. Mary Ann Crabtree died in 1905, and Lotta became increasingly aloof. She resurfaced for one final public appearance in San Francisco, in honor of the Panama-Pacific Exposition of 1915 having scheduled an official Lotta Crabtree Day. Residents turned out by the thousands to pay tribute to "our Lotta."

Returning to the East Coast, Lotta left New Jersey and purchased the Brewster Hotel in Boston, where she spent the rest of her life. A residence hall at the nearby University of Massachusetts, Amherst, is named "Charlotte M. Crabtree Hall" in her honor.

Lotta Crabtree died in 1924 at age seventy-six, leaving an estate estimated in excess of $4 million. In keeping with earlier philanthropic work, her will left the bulk of the money to needy World War I veterans, aging actors, various animal charities, and a trust for young people's education in music and agriculture.

Her obituaries frequently echoed a phrase used by critics during her heyday: Lotta Crabtree was "like no one in the world."

SIERRA SPOTLIGHT

Kate and Ellen Bateman

Participants in the California Gold Rush were often far from home and hearth, and they understandably craved the sights and sounds of families they had left behind. The largely male audiences were drawn to women like Lola Montez for obvious reasons, but they also enjoyed performances by child stars like Lotta Crabtree, perhaps because she reminded them of daughters or sisters they longed to see. Among the more prominent child actors were Kate and Ellen Batemen, aged eleven and nine, respectively, in 1853. The pair widely and frequently performed dramatic scenes in both male and female roles, most notably as Macbeth and Lady Macbeth, Shylock and Portia, and Richard III and Richmond, all in full adult wardrobe, including mustaches.

Playbill featuring the popular child actresses Ellen and Kate Bateman as characters in Shakespeare's *Richard III*, c. 1850. Engraving by Hollis from a daguerreotype by Mayall. Courtesy of the Folger Shakespeare Library, Washington, DC, ART File B328.5 no. 1 (size XS).

NORTH FORK, AMERICAN RIVER, CALIFORNIA.

SACAGAWEA'S SON

The Adventures of Pompy

The city of Auburn is one of the few places that combines every major theme of the chronicle of the American West. It is there, in Placer County, that we see the mingling of the histories of the westward movement (Auburn is on a tentacle of the California Trail); of the Transcontinental Railroad (the city is a major stop on the route); of the Gold Rush; and, perhaps surprisingly, of the Lewis and Clark Expedition. Just as interesting is that all of these threads are also connected through a single person who lived and worked in the foothill community—an individual known as Pompy.

Jean Baptiste Charbonneau, Sacagawea's son, spent most of his adult life in Auburn, Placer County, on the North Fork of the American River. Engraving by Gleason, 1854. Printed in *Gleason's Pictorial: Scenes in California*, Boston, March 25, 1854. From the California History Room Picture Collection: Prints F-Size: Mines and Mining: Gold: Placer County, no. 2008-3305, courtesy of the California State Library, Sacramento.

His actual name was Jean Baptiste Charbonneau, and although we have little information about him as an adult, we know a lot about him as a child. He was born in North Dakota in 1805 and was the son of Sacagawea, a Shoshone woman who served as a guide for the Lewis and Clark Expedition (1804–1806). His father, the French Canadian trapper Toussaint Charbonneau, was an interpreter on the trip.

Jean Baptiste's birth is quite likely the best-documented delivery in the history of the nineteenth-century American West. To modern audiences, it may also seem the most unusual. On February 11, 1805, Meriwether Lewis, one of the co-commanders of the Corps of Discovery, as the expedition was called, recorded the nativity in his journal:

> About five oclock this evening one of the wives of Charbono
> was delivered of a fine boy. It is worthy of remark that this
> was the first child which this woman had boarn and as is
> common in such cases her labour was tedious and the pain
> violent; Mr. Jessome informed me that he had freequently
> adminstered a small portion of the rattle of the rattle-snake,
> which he assured me had never failed to produce the desired
> effect, that of hastening the birth of the child; having the
> rattle of a snake by me I gave it to him and he administered
> two rings of it to the woman broken in small pieces with
> the fingers and added to a small quantity of water. Whether
> this medicine was truly the cause or not I shall not under-
> take to determine, but I was informed that she had not
> taken it more than ten minutes before she brought forth[;]
> perhaps this remedy may be worthy of future experiments,
> but I must confess that I want faith as to its efficacy.

The rattlesnake-induced infant was nicknamed Little Pomp or Pompy by William Clark, the other leader of the famous party. Pompy traveled with his young mother on the expedition, often carried on her back. Not only was the journey difficult for the newborn but he also contracted an illness that could easily have turned deadly in those days of primitive medical care. Suffering from what is believed to have been either mumps or tonsillitis, the baby had a high fever and a swollen neck and throat. The members of the Corps of Discovery did what they could to alleviate the child's discomfort, but the boy was not improving. Lewis wrote in his journal a few days later that little Pomp "was very wrestless last night; it's jaw and back of it's neck are much more swolen…we gave it a doze of creem of tartar and applied a fresh poltice of onions." The child slowly recovered, and many historians have noted that the baby's presence was reassuring to the natives, as he underscored the expedition's peaceful intentions.

Today, Pompy's image can be found on the Sacagawea dollar coin. The infant rests happily on his mother's back. He is the only child ever to have been depicted on American currency.

In 1809, several years after the conclusion of the expedition, little Pompy went to live with William Clark, who resided in St. Louis while his parents set out on a new excursion. Clark paid for the boy's education, including schooling in Missouri. In 1823, at age eighteen, Pompy, now preferring to be called Jean Baptiste, was working at an Indian trading post near Kansas City when he met a royal visitor from Germany: Duke Friedrich Paul Wilhelm of Württemberg. The duke was on a natural history expedition in the Great Plains, for which Jean Baptiste's itinerant father was a guide. The duke invited Jean Baptiste to return to Europe as his guest, and the now not-so-little Pompy accepted and spent the next six years traveling throughout Europe and northern Africa.

In 1829, Jean Baptiste returned to the United States to work as a fur trapper and hunting guide. William Boggs, a tourist, described him as a character who "wore his hair long, [and] was…very high strung" and, Boggs continued, "it was said Charbenau was the best man on foot on the plains or in the Rocky Mountains."

After years of trapping, guiding, and scouting, Charbonneau was appointed as alcalde (mayor) of Mission San Luis Rey de Francia, where he served for less than a year before resigning his post in August 1848 due to political tensions.

In September 1848, during the giddy first day of the Gold Rush, he arrived in Placer County at the camp known as North Fork Dry Diggings and settled near Secret Ravine, one of twelve ravines in and around Auburn. He was a semi-successful miner at this ravine and several others in the region; the 1882 *History of Placer County* said his Auburn claim "was shallow and paid well." Charbonneau resided in Auburn for the next sixteen years, and worked as the hotel manager of the Orleans Hotel in Old Town, having quickly realized that mining was a notoriously fickle pursuit and that to survive in a Gold Rush town a man was wise to have another occupation.

In April 1866, Charbonneau left Auburn for Montana. The *Placer Herald* reported that his purpose was "returning to familiar scenes" in the Great Basin, but he had more likely gone to prospect for gold. Only a few weeks later, on May 16, 1866, Charbonneau died en route to eastern Oregon. Reports were unclear as to the cause of the death, although it seems the sixty-one-year-old contracted a fatal disease. His obituary in the *Placer Herald* said he succumbed to "Mountain Fever," a rapidly debilitating viral infection transmitted by ticks.

Jean Baptiste Charbonneau is buried near Danner, Oregon, at a spot listed on the National Register of Historic Places and marked by several monuments erected by historical societies, civic organizations, and Native American groups. In Auburn, he is honored with a memorial plaque resting in the shade of a cedar tree near the Old Firehouse.

SIERRA SPOTLIGHT

Joseph B. Starkweather

Although no pictures of the adult Jean Baptiste Charbonneau are known to exist, we are fortunate to possess a wealth of imagery from his era. The California Gold Rush coincided with the birth of photography, and early practitioners provided many fascinating depictions of the Age of Gold. Perhaps the most iconic and widely reproduced images of the Gold Rush are those attributed to Joseph Blaney Starkweather, a daguerreotypist from Massachusetts who may have been the actual photographer or might also have been simply the publisher of the images credited to him. The Starkweather daguerreotypes show life in the spare, unsentimental goldfields of 1850 through 1852 and are especially valuable as they show members of the society that were rare or not commonly depicted, including African American and Chinese miners and, most notably, women, the rarest of all Gold Rush participants. The original Starkweather daguerreotypes are extremely fragile and are safely stored in a special vault deep in the recesses of the California State Library in Sacramento.

"Spanish Flat, 1852," a Gold Rush daguerreotype attributed to Joseph B. Stark-weather, 1852. From the California History Room, Daguerreotype V: Mines and Mining: Gold: Scenes from Daguerreotype S#1: Spanish Flat, 1852, no. DAG-0100. Courtesy of the California State Library, Sacramento.

904. The Mother of the Forest, 305 feet high,

JUST TO PROVE A POINT

Fall of the Forest Monarchs

In the nineteenth century, rumors abounded of the wonders of the American West. Eager listeners heard tell of solid gold mountains, waterfalls that flowed upward, and even claims that dinosaurs still wandered the hills and valleys. In an era of limited communications, these stories were sometimes hard to prove, and in response the public often adopted a "show me" attitude. It was this way of thinking that led to the tragic toppling of many of California's giant sequoias, the Big Trees of the Sierra.

Starting with the arrival of European Americans on the West Coast in the 1840s, these monarchs of the forest—gargantuan trees reaching hundreds of feet into the sky and growing dozens of feet in diameter—became featured characters in reports of the exotic California landscape. "Show me," said the skeptics. "Prove your claim." And so

The scarred remains of "The Mother of the Forest" in the Calaveras Big Trees. Photograph by Lawrence and Houseworth, c. 1865. From the Lawrence and Houseworth Collection, courtesy of the Society of California Pioneers, Image #694 (SCP).

began the practice of cutting down specimens of *Sequoiadendron giganteum*, among other impressive species, to provide tangible evidence for the unbelieving.

This smaller-scale destruction was augmented by a thriving and cruelly efficient lumber industry in the Sierra Nevada. Timber was needed for the mines and the development of the railroad, and it was not long before lumbering became a significant force in the regional economy. In 1858, Nevada County, for example, had forty-two lumber mills that produced more than 39 million feet of lumber in one calendar year. Thirteen lumber mills were located in Grass Valley alone. Multiply that by the counties that stretch throughout the Sierra for a sense of the scope of the endeavor. A 1924 Stanford University report stated that the number of lumber mills in California increased from 80 in 1855 to 320 in 1860—the vast majority of which were concentrated in the western counties of the northern and central Sierra Nevada—and a California State Forestry Board Report estimated that by 1886, after nearly twenty years of intense lumber production and fire, a full one-third of the Sierra Nevada's timber resources had been "consumed and destroyed."

The lumber industry of this era followed practices that ranged from careless and wasteful to enduringly harmful. Trees were cut at a convenient height for those doing the cutting but with no regard for the unsightly landscape of three-foot-tall stumps they had created. Other times, lumberjacks would fell trees but haul out only the limbless bottom parts, leaving the upper branches behind to often become fuel for devastating fires that consumed nearby quality timber. Sawmills generated thousands of tons of sawdust, which was frequently dumped into adjacent rivers, killing fish and damaging water quality. Log transport in the rivers themselves scoured the streambeds, injuring riparian habitat. In 1888, John Muir noted on his trip up the Truckee River to Lake Tahoe that the river canyon was littered with "fallen burnt logs or the tops of trees felled for lumber." The industry was relentless.

Now, to cut down a tree in the name of commerce was one thing, but to take on the felling of a tree as huge as a giant sequoia was another. It was, unfortunately, a challenge embraced by a generation that believed conquering nature was not only possible but desirable.

Giant sequoias are the largest living organisms on the planet, and among the oldest. Some tower more than two hundred feet, have diameters in excess of thirty feet, and are thousands of years old. The General Sherman Tree, in Sequoia National Park, is generally believed to be the world's largest life form; it is 275 feet tall, 37 feet in diameter, contains an estimated 52,500 cubic feet of lumber, and is about 2,400 years old.

Among the first of these monarchs to fall were those in the Calaveras Big Trees, a famous grove of giant sequoias located in lush woodlands near the rapidly flowing North Fork of the Stanislaus River, about twenty-five miles east of Angels Camp. Credit for the "discovery" of the Big Trees was given to Augustus Dowd in 1852, although earlier records challenge the claim. (An entry in John Bidwell's 1841 diary mentions "an enormous fallen tree" in the area, and one trunk in the grove bears the carved graffiti "L.M. Wooster June 1850.") Of course, native Californians had most likely seen the trees long before these dates, but Dowd's testimony endures as one of the earliest public accounts. James Hutchings, editor and publisher of *Hutchings' California Magazine*, reported in 1859 that Dowd was alone when he first spied the Big Trees while chasing a wounded bear. When he attempted to describe the scene to his hunting companions, they laughed at him, "supposing that he was trying to perpetuate upon them some first-of-April joke." But when his buddies finally arrived at the giant sequoia grove their "doubt was changed into certainty, and unbelief into amazement; as, speechless with profound awe, their admiring gaze was riveted upon these forest giants." After that, word spread quickly; as Hutchings recalled, "a short season was...to elapse before the trumpet-tongued press proclaimed the wonders; and worshippers flocked to the Big Trees to see for themselves the astounding marvels about which they had heard so much."

The Calaveras Big Trees prominently feature the famous Discovery Tree Stump, the remnant of a tree cut down to create a twenty-five-foot-diameter dance floor out of the base. It was supposedly the first giant sequoia seen by Augustus Dowd, but by the following year, five workers had spent several weeks severing the massive tree. Since standard saws were ineffective on an object so large, the lumbermen drilled through the tree with augers. Even then, because the tree was perfectly symmetrical and well balanced, it took a strong breeze to finally topple the sequoia.

In 1859, James Hutchings described the stump as "perfectly smooth, sound and level," and he was astonished that "upon this stump, however incredible it may seem, on the 4th of July, 32 persons were engaged in dancing four sets of cotillions at one time, without suffering any inconvenience whatever; and besides these, there were musicians and lookers on." But even Hutchings, perhaps the greatest huckster for Sierra Nevada tourism who ever lived, found this monumental destruction to be "a sacrilegious act" and an "act of desecration." John Muir famously denounced this sorrowful artifact in his 1901 book *Our National Parks*:

> Great trees and groves used to be venerated as sacred monuments and halls of council and worship. But soon after the discovery of the Calaveras Grove one of the grandest trees was cut down for the sake of a stump! The laborious vandals had seen 'the biggest tree in the world,' then, forsooth, they must try to see the biggest stump and dance on it.

The huge chunk of fallen timber still rests alongside its stump. At one point its surface was used as a bowling alley. Early on, a tourist pavilion was constructed atop the stump and the structure was used as a dance hall, newspaper office, and exhibit room. A nearby piece of the prostrate trunk, nicknamed "The Chip," had a ladder attached that for years allowed visitors to climb the remnant. The pavilion and the ladder have since been dismantled and the tree is protected as part of the state park.

Another poignant vestige in the Calaveras Big Trees grove is the enormous charred stump of a giant sequoia made famous when its bark was removed in 1854. In that year, George Trask had 116 feet of bark stripped from one of the largest trees in the area, named "Mother of the Forest." This herculean task took four workers a total of twenty-one days to accomplish. Hutchings described the process in an 1859 magazine article titled "The Mammoth Trees of California":

To the first branch is 137 feet [above ground]. The small
black marks upon the tree indicate points where 2 ½ in.
auger holes were bored, into which rounds were inserted,
by which to ascend and descend while removing the bark.
At different distances upward, and especially at the top,
numerous dates, and names of visitors, have been carved.
It is contemplated to construct a circular stairway around
the tree. While the bark was being removed a young man
fell from the scaffolding…at a distance of 79 feet from the
ground, and escaped with a broken limb. We were within
a few yards of him when he fell, and we were agreeably
surprised to discover that he had not broken his neck.

The detached bark was reassembled for a traveling exhibit designed
to prove the existence of these gigantic wonders (and to make some
money, of course). The massive artifact was presented throughout the
United States and ultimately ended up in England. In London, the reconstructed tree bark was displayed in a glass case in the Crystal Palace;
an elaborate Victorian structure originally built for the Great Exhibition
of 1851 and then itself dismantled and rebuilt in a new location. A fire
destroyed the sequoia bark in 1866 and today the only remnant of this
sad incident is the bare Mother of the Forest trunk, still ringed with the
small black holes drilled generations ago, and now many times a target
for lightning and fire, left to slowly decay like a broken tooth.

The General Noble Tree

In 1893, the official exhibit of the United States Pavilion at the Chicago World's Fair was a thirty-foot-tall hollow section of a giant sequoia from Kings Canyon, named the General Noble Tree, in honor of John Willock Noble, Secretary of the Interior from 1889 to 1893. The General Noble was severed nearly fifty feet above ground level, and when the immense one-thousand-ton trunk fell, it took down the scaffolding and nearly killed the loggers. Four men at the top of the scaffolding leaped onto the fifty-foot stump and grabbed a precarious handhold as the base vibrated wildly for a reported twenty minutes. In this case, since the exhibitors were only interested in the stump, the remainder of the giant trunk was split into garden stakes and fence posts. A thirty-five-foot section of the stump was configured into a two-story hollow structure equipped with an interior staircase and capped with an ornately gabled roof. The floor separating the two stories was a fat slice of the sequoia itself. Visitors could enter for a small fee. The government's reasoning for felling this beautiful organism was to once and for all prove the existence of the fabled Big Trees to a doubting public back East. Following the fair, the "tree house" was transferred to the National Mall in Washington, DC, near the Smithsonian Castle, where it remained as a gardener's shed until 1932.

The General Noble Tree House from the Old Agriculture Building in Washington, DC, c.1930. In the distance are the Smithsonian Castle and the US Capitol. From the Historic Images of the Smithsonian Collection, courtesy of the Smithsonian Institution, Washington, DC, MAH-61694.

A PERILOUS TRIP—SHOOTING A FLUME IN THE SIERRA NEVADA.—Drawn by Graham and Day.—[See Page 477.]

THE ULTIMATE THRILL

The Great Flume Ride of 1875

Lumber was a highly desired commodity during the Gold Rush, and demand continued to surge in the 1870s with an increase in railroad construction and underground mining. On the Sierra Nevada Railroad mainline, the building of the summit snow sheds alone required 300 million board feet of lumber, with another 20 million needed annually for maintenance. Nevada's Comstock Lode used more than 70 million board feet for its silver and gold mines, and that was just one strike. The burgeoning regional population needed millions more board feet every year for building homes, businesses, and fences, and of course there was demand for lumber from throughout California and beyond.

How did the industry transport lumber across mountain ridges to places far away? A common solution was the construction of flumes: V-shaped troughs that used running water to move the lumber. At least

"A Perilous Trip," an illustration from *Harper's Weekly*, June 2, 1877. Courtesy of The Bancroft Library, University of California, Berkeley, AP2 H3 v. 21, pp. 428–429.

ten flumes spread like a spider web through the Lake Tahoe and Carson Valley regions. Many modern-day Tahoe visitors may be familiar with the Old Flume Trail, a popular hiking and biking path that runs fifteen miles along the Nevada side of the lake following the route of a flume that has since been dismantled.

The most interesting and influential flume has largely been forgotten, its route nearly impossible to find, having being swallowed by time and vegetation. The Bonanza V was located about twenty miles north of Lake Tahoe, beginning near Hunter Lake and plummeting roughly fifteen miles eastward to Huffaker's Station, a stop on the Virginia and Truckee Railroad, south of Reno. It is here that the next story unfolds.

The Bonanza V was the creation of the Pacific Wood, Lumber, and Flume Company, a business built by a group of mine owners to provide lumber for the up-and-coming needs of the Comstock Lode, near Virginia City, Nevada. Most notable among the company stockholders were James C. Flood, James G. Fair, John Mackay, and William S. O'Brien, all principal mine owners in the Comstock Lode region. These four fabulously wealthy characters had, to use a common phrase of the day, "seen their opportunities and took 'em."

Back in 1857, James Flood opened a saloon with partner William S. O'Brien in San Francisco, but by 1858 they had tired of barkeeping, sold the saloon, and gone into business selling stock. After Henry Comstock's discovery of silver in western Nevada in 1859, Flood and O'Brien began investing in mining stocks. Reaping immediate profits, Flood and O'Brien formed a partnership in 1860 with James Graham Fair, a mine superintendent, and John William Mackay, a mining engineer. These dynamic business partners soon controlled and operated the Virginia and California claims in the Comstock Lode under the company name Consolidated Virginia Mining Company.

Mackay and Fair brought their mining knowledge to the table while Flood and O'Brien were the financial wizards. The purchase price of their claims was about $100,000 and the original stock issue was 10,700 shares, selling for about $5 per share. In 1873, the greatest silver strike in history occurred in Virginia City. It was called the "Big Bonanza," and the extraordinary silver ore deposit was more than 1,200 feet deep and yielded as much as $632 per ton. The company's mining stock soared in value, with individual shares selling for nearly $710. Within two years, the overall value of the Consolidated Virginia Mining Company was more than $1 billion. During the first half of 1875, the output of the mines averaged $1.5 million per month.

Virginia City became a boomtown as, within weeks, thousands of prospectors descended upon the desert community. A commercial section rose rapidly and soon there were hotels, restaurants, shops, saloons, boarding houses, and even an opera house. But there was a problem: Virginia City was miles away from the nearest forest, and builders would be hard pressed to find a usable stick of wood in the local area. Yet all this mining and civic development required stupendous amounts of timber. What to do? The solution was to harvest timber from the nearby Lake Tahoe Basin, about thirty miles away, and transport it to Virginia City, an effort that would require hundreds of employees, train tracks, horses, wagons, and a network of flumes.

The Bonanza V flume was constructed for the then-astronomical sum of nearly $300,000, but Flood estimated that the flume saved his company nearly $500,000 annually in transportation costs. It was an expensive but cost-effective investment. The flume snaked through the mountains north of Lake Tahoe on a trestle that ranged from twenty to seventy feet above the ground and dropped a total of 1,750 feet in elevation. Constructed in only ten weeks, the flume used two million feet of lumber and twenty-eight tons of nails. Finished, it moved approximately five hundred thousand feet of lumber per day—an amount that would have otherwise required about two thousand horses to accomplish.

In 1875, reporter H. J. Ramsdell of the *New York Tribune* was invited by James Flood and James Fair to visit the Bonanza V flume and then dared to take a ride along its length. Ramsdell accepted the challenge, and two flume boats were brought forth. Ramsdell commented on the boats in an 1876 article for the *Williams' Pacific Tourist* magazine:

> These were nothing more than pig-troughs, with one end
> knocked out. The 'boat' is built, like the flume, V shaped,

and fits into the flume. It is composed of three pieces of wood—two two-inch planks, 16 feet long, and an end board which is nailed about two and one-half feet across the top. The forward end of the boat was left open, the rear end closed with a board—against which was to come the current of water to propel us. Two narrow boards were placed in the boat for seats.

Ramsdell insisted the owners take the ride as well. James Fair, the reporter, and a plucky volunteer whom Ramsdell described as "a red-faced carpenter, who takes more kindly to whisky than his bench," were in the first boat, and James Flood and John Hereford, the superintendent of the flume, were in the second. Interested bystanders yelled "Hang on to your hats" and, as Ramsdell recalled, "The signal of 'all ready' was given, the boat was launched, and we jumped into it as best we could, which was not very well, and away we went like the wind."

Ramsdell was petrified:

> The terrors of that ride can never be blotted from the memory….[Y]ou can not go fast or slow at pleasure; you are wholly at the mercy of the water. You can not stop; you can not lessen your speed; you have nothing to hold to; you have only to sit still, shut your eyes, say your prayers, take all water that comes—filling your boat, wetting your feet, drenching you like a plunge through the surf,—and wait for eternity. It is all there is to hope for after you are launched in a flume-boat.

At times the flume had a 45-degree inclination. As Ramsdell explained:

> In this ride…I was perched up in a boat no wider than a chair, sometimes 20 feet high in the air, and with the ever varying altitude of the flume, often 70 feet high. When the water would enable me to look ahead, I would see this trestle here and there for miles, so small and narrow, and apparently so fragile, that I could only compare it to a chalk-mark, upon which, high in the air, I was running at a rate unknown upon railroads.

The boats careened wildly from side to side. At one point, the daring reporter recalled:

> We had been rushing down at a pretty lively rate of speed, when the boat suddenly struck something in the bow—a nail, or lodged stick of wood, which ought not to have been there. What was the result? The red-faced carpenter was sent whirling into the flume, 10 feet ahead. Fair was precipitated on his face, and I found a soft lodgment on Fair's back.

Sopping wet and hurtling along in a seemingly unstoppable rocket, Ramsdell found the experience alternately spine-tingling and horrifying, and the speed was beyond human understanding:

> How our boat kept in the track is more than I know. The wind, the steamboat, the railroad never went so fast….If the truth must be spoken, I was really scared almost out of reason; but if I was on the way to eternity, I wanted to know exactly how fast I went; so I… turned my eyes toward the hills. Every object I placed my eye on was gone, before I could clearly see what it was. Mountains passed like visions and shadows.

They zoomed along at speeds that James Fair estimated at sixty miles per hour but which James Flood figured had to be one hundred miles per hour. Ramsdell had his own opinion: "My deliberate belief is that we went at a rate that annihilated time and space."

Flood's estimate of one hundred miles per hour is an understandable exaggeration. His boat caught the Ramsdell/Fair vessel during the perilous ride and slammed into its rear. Flood fell on his face and the waters engulfed him, drenching him thoroughly. Flood's fellow passenger, Superintendent Hereford, was also saturated and scared stiff.

Finally, the intrepid voyagers reached the end of the flume after less than thirty minutes. (Ramsdell said it felt like hours.) Wet and shaken, they assessed their journey. James Flood declared he would never make the trip again, even for all the value of his mine holdings. James Fair, whose fingers had been severely pinched between the boat and the flume in the crash, exclaimed that he "should never again place himself on an equality with timber and wood," and John Hereford said he was sorry that he ever built the damn thing. "As for myself," Ramsdell declared, "I told the millionaires that I had accepted my last challenge. When we left we were more dead than alive."

The next day, back in Virginia City, neither James Flood nor James Fair were able to leave their beds. As for H. J. Ramsdell, his feelings were very clear: "For myself, I only had strength enough left to say, 'I have had enough of flumes.'"

Today, lumber is moved by more efficient means of transportation and log flumes are the stuff of amusement parks, although none gives as harrowing a ride as the Bonanza V did in 1875.

SIERRA SPOTLIGHT

The Incline

One solution for transporting Sierra lumber in the late nineteenth century was the construction of a massive tram railway on the east shore of Lake Tahoe. Called "The Incline," it was completed in 1880 by the Sierra Nevada Wood and Lumber Company. The Incline elevated lumber from its associated lakeside mill upward to a flume that ultimately delivered the wood for use in the Comstock mines and Virginia City. The location of the Incline is preserved by the name of the community that was built on the spot—Incline Village.

The original Incline was dismantled after years of use, but the location became part of popular culture in the 1960s when it was featured on the television series *Bonanza*. The incline area was part of the Ponderosa, the huge landholding of the fictional Cartwright clan, and in 1967, the site became the location of the Ponderosa Ranch, an amusement theme park built to capitalize on *Bonanza*. Ponderosa Ranch closed its doors in 2004, but sharp-eyed observers can still see the fading path of the Incline, which once rose from its parking lot.

The Sierra Nevada Wood and Lumber Company's Incline on the north shore of Lake Tahoe. Photograph by R. J. Waters, c. 1885. From the Braun Research Collection, courtesy of the Autry National Center, Los Angeles, P-13162.

TWENTY-THREE MILES IN SEVEN DAYS

The 1911 Tahoe Tavern Automobile Race

At the turn of the twentieth century most roads in the Sierra were treacherous, not to be traveled by the faint of heart. In 1901 the Bureau of Highways described the skinny tentacle over Sonora Pass as "22 miles over granite formation that is little more than a creek bed." One wag depicted another highway as so muddy in winter and spring that it measured "130 miles long and 5 feet deep." Even when funding became available for mountain road construction and repair, costs were prohibitive, the traffic skimpy, and the Sierra work season too brief to justify the effort. As a result, the state diverted most of its highway funds to populated areas, relegating Sierra Nevada roads

The intrepid adventurers of the 1911 Tahoe Tavern Automobile Race drag their vehicle over a snow bank at Donner Pass. Courtesy of the Searls Historical Library, Nevada County Historical Society, Nevada City, California, PIC5-TRA-AUTO-35.

to afterthoughts. Driving a car through the range in the first fifteen years of the twentieth century was an adventure for sure, and also potentially deadly.

Evidence is sketchy as to what should be considered the first automobile to crest the Sierra, but one convincing account reports that a party of "autoists," as they were charmingly called, successfully crossed Donner Pass in May 1901. The next year, audacious Oakland native George Wyman became the first motorcyclist to accomplish the feat as part of his historic journey to become the first person to cross the United States by motor vehicle, which he did in fifty-one days—twenty days faster than Dr. Horatio Nelson Jackson and Sewall K. Crocker, who in 1903 became the first people to drive an automobile across the United States.

Perhaps the most remarkable automobile passage over the Sierra Nevada was the result of a contest. In spring of 1911, the Tahoe Tavern in Tahoe City offered a three-foot-tall silver trophy to the first party to drive eastward over the Donner Summit Road from California to the luxury resort. The Sierra had just endured a severe winter—by March of that year nearly forty feet of snow had fallen at 8,000 feet—so it was not until June that anyone dared attempt the exhilarating but arduous race over the trackless, snowy Sierra.

The leading contenders for the prize were a dedicated group of automobile fanatics from Grass Valley led by Arthur B. Foote, assistant superintendent of the North Star Mines Corporation. Joining him on the ride was George Starr, manager of the Empire Mine. They expected brutal physical challenges on the trip, including difficult terrain and serious logistical issues that would require pushing, pulling, and perhaps carrying their auto over obstacles, but they did not anticipate that it would take them seven days to travel the last twenty-three miles.

Just a few years earlier, in 1908, Foote had purchased his first automobile, a Model T Ford. It was delivered to him in parts, which he assembled himself, thereby becoming quickly and hopelessly devoted to his homemade motor vehicle. When Foote learned of the Tahoe Tavern contest, he instantly decided to undertake the competition in his prized possession and recruited Starr and other Grass Valley citizens as his support crew.

On June 2, 1911, Foote and Starr began their journey. Foote, true to his roots as a mining engineer, kept an understated, even terse, diary. His first entry reads: "Packed stuff, took off windshield, Mr. Starr and I left for Emigrant Gap at 4 p.m. with shovels, tackle, etc. Passed Emigrant Gap and got stuck in the soft snow 2.5 miles further on. Walked to Cisco, got there 10:30 p.m."

Snow blocked their way that night, so the following morning Foote and Starr went scouting. They walked their potential route and discovered a washed-out bridge on the roaring Yuba River. Hiking back to their automobile in Cisco, the intrepid pair started driving across the still-frozen snowpack. Occasionally, the automobile would careen into deep crevices and Foote and Starr would need to haul their car out of the holes using a block and tackle. After five hours, they finally reached the washed-out bridge, at which point they stretched a metal cable over the torrent, cleverly slid the suspended car over the rapids, and then quickly removed the cable, leaving no evidence of the ingenious technique for the competitors that followed. When their opponents reached the ruined bridge, they were puzzled as to how Foote and Starr had crossed. They were also unable to continue. With an overwhelming lead, the dynamic duo from Grass Valley continued onward.

Two days later, Foote and Starr were once again stuck in the snow, but, still confident that success was within reach, they returned to Grass Valley by train to retrieve more equipment before pressing on. On June 7, they were back with their stranded auto, which they yanked into position and fitted with wooden runners on the wheels. The car now turned into a sled, the adventurers pushed it over the snowpack, and by June 9, they had reached Soda Springs, where they spent the day making repairs. The next morning, Foote and Starr pulled their vehicle over Donner Summit and then manhandled it to Donner Lake, where they enjoyed a well-earned breakfast. With nothing left but the open road from Truckee to Tahoe City, the triumphant contestants reached Tahoe Tavern at noon. Overall, the outing had taken eight days. The three-foot-tall trophy was theirs, and so were bragging rights.

The Tahoe Tavern proprietors were astonished to see Arthur Foote and George Starr. On June 11, the *Grass Valley Union* reported on the front page: "The victors enjoyed the consternation which they caused by their unexpected arrival. The resort management had not expected these men from Grass Valley to achieve their success by shoving, tugging, and hoisting their Model T over seemingly impassable mountainous terrain."

SIERRA SPOTLIGHT

Alice Huyler Ramsey

In 1909, Alice Huyler Ramsey became the first woman to drive across the United States. The twenty-two-year-old New Jersey housewife and Vassar College graduate was accompanied by three other women, none of whom knew how to drive. Beginning in Manhattan, the trip took fifty-nine days and covered 3,800 miles, of which only 152 were paved. Driving a brand-new green Maxwell 30 automobile, Ramsey changed eleven tires, repaired a broken brake pedal, cleaned the spark plugs, and suffered from a case of bedbugs. In 1961, she wrote an account of her trip entitled *Veil, Duster, and Tire Iron.*

After a brief respite in Sparks Nevada, having just crossed the sizzling Great Basin in the July heat, Alice's Great Adventure continued as she and her three companions crested the Sierra Nevada near Lake Tahoe. It took the quartet eight hours to travel seventy miles, and Alice recalled her emotions upon reaching the summit: "Majestic sugar pines, Douglas firs and redwoods lined our roads on both sides. What a land! What mountains! What blue skies and clear, sparkling water! Our hearts leapt within us. None of us had ever seen the like—and we loved it. We almost chirped as we exclaimed over the grandeur that surrounded us on all sides."

In October 2000, Alice Huyler Ramsey became the first woman inducted into the Automotive Hall of Fame, in Dearborn, Michigan.

Alice Huyler Ramsey, the first woman to drive across the United States, c. 1910. From the George Grantham Bain Collection, c. 1900, courtesy of the Library of Congress, Prints and Photographs Division, Washington, DC, LC-DIG-ggbain-03065.

CAMEL TRAIN IN NEVADA.—Drawn by Frenzeny.—[See Page 502.]

CURIOUS CARAVAN

Edward Fitzgerald Beale and the Camel Corps

Perhaps the most exotic form of transportation in the Sierra Nevada was the use of camels in the 1850s and 60s. Much of the history of this colorful conveyance revolves around Edward Fitzgerald Beale, one of the most accomplished yet largely overlooked figures of the nineteenth-century American West.

Beale had been an important figure on the national scene for many years, having received appointments and commissions from five United States presidents, beginning with Andrew Jackson and concluding with Ulysses S. Grant. He was a lieutenant in the Navy, an anti-British spy, a veteran of the Mexican War, the Superintendent of Indian Affairs for California and Nevada, the Surveyor General of California, a brigadier general in the California State Militia, and an ambassador to Austria-Hungary. He counted among his many friends such lively characters as

Edward Fitzgerald Beale's Camel Corps in Nevada, an illustration by Frenzeny from *Harper's Weekly*, June 30, 1877. Courtesy of The Bancroft Library, University of California, Berkeley, p. 501.

Kit Carson, John C. Frémont's scout; the flamboyant showman Buffalo Bill Cody; Civil War hero General William Tecumseh Sherman; and Emperor Franz Josef I of Austria-Hungary.

In 1848, Beale was responsible for providing physical proof to the federal government in Washington, DC, that gold had indeed been discovered in California. Having collected a bag of samples, Beale's journey back East required him to enter Mexican territory, through which he scurried stealthily in a disguise, no doubt calling upon his skills as a former undercover agent. Back in California, in 1865 and 1866 Beale used some of his vast wealth to purchase Tejon Ranch, a group of Mexican land grants that totaled 270,000 acres—real estate almost twice the size of the City and County of San Francisco.

Beale's adventures were many and varied, but the most bizarre entry on his impressive résumé is undoubtedly his role as commander of the first and only camel expedition in United States military history.

As early as 1836, the United States War Department had toyed with importing camels as a means of transport in the arid regions of the country. In 1848, with the discovery of gold in California, the concept of utilizing camels for frontier military service gained momentum. An early supporter was Jefferson Davis, the future President of the Confederacy during the Civil War, but then a senator from Mississippi. In 1853, Davis became the secretary of war and gave his full backing to the experimental Camel Corps. In a report to President Franklin Pierce on December 1, 1853, Davis urged the government to import the camels:

> For military purposes, for expresses, and for reconnaissances, it is believed, the dromedary [camel] would supply a want now seriously felt in our service; and for transportation with troops rapidly moving across the country, the camel, it is believed, would remove an obstacle which now serves greatly to diminish the value of efficiency of our troops on the western frontier.

Congress did not act immediately, and Davis again appealed for funding to test the animals' capabilities in Western terrain and weather conditions. On March 3, 1855, a bill was finally passed appropriating

$30,000 for a camel experiment. Among those strongly voicing public support was Edward Fitzgerald Beale, then Superintendent of Indian Affairs in California and Nevada.

In mid-1855, the store-ship USS *Supply* was dispatched to the Middle East to purchase a load of camels. The following September, the *Supply* was loaded with thirty-three camels, including one so tall that a hole had to be cut in the roof of the cargo bay to allow enough space for its hump. The ship, which was also carrying five camel drivers from the Middle East, arrived in Texas in spring of 1856, and was soon after ordered to return to Egypt to secure more camels for the experiment.

All the camels—seventy in total—arrived in Camp Verde, Texas, on August 26, 1857. Beale was chosen to head the expedition as part of his assignment from President James Buchanan to survey and construct a 1,000-mile road from New Mexico to California. (Beale took it upon himself to extend the California terminus to his property at Fort Tejon, near today's Bakersfield.) Beale used the camels as pack animals during this effort, and from all accounts, the camels acquitted themselves admirably—traveling days without water, carrying much heavier loads than horses and mules, and surviving on the available rough forage that other animals would not touch.

In January 1858, to test the camels' adaptability to cold conditions, Beale established a camp high in the southern Sierra. He reported in his journal:

> I had placed [the camels] in camp within a few hundred
> yards of the summit of the Sierra Nevada, and to this
> date they had lived in two or three feet of snow, fattening
> and thriving wonderfully all the while. Lately, in a ter-
> rible snowstorm, the wagon, carrying provisions to the
> camp, could proceed no further. The camels were imme-
> diately sent to the rescue, and brought the load through
> the snow and ice to camp, though the six strong mules
> of the team were unable to extricate the empty wagon.

Upon reaching California and his home at Fort Tejon, Beale and the War Department assessed the Camel Corps experiment. Most agreed the camels had commendable and useful qualities. Despite evidence that the camels were not compatible with other animals and sometimes scared the soldiers, Beale suggested the experiment continue, and in 1858, the new secretary of war, John B. Floyd, recommended the government purchase an additional one thousand camels immediately. Floyd's multiple requests were rejected in 1858, 1859, and 1860, and then the beginning of the Civil War permanently ended the military exercise.

Beale kept a few of the camels at his Fort Tejon ranch, but many were sold at auction. A small number of the camels became circus performers and a handful were used for racing, but most served as pack animals for private firms. It is likely that some camels were simply released into the Nevada desert, and by the 1870s wild camels had become such a nuisance that the state legislature passed an act in February 1875 prohibiting "camels and dromedaries from running at large on or about the public highways of the State of Nevada."

SIERRA SPOTLIGHT

Otto Esche's Camel Express

Following the dissolution of the US government's Camel Corps, the exotic animals made a brief comeback in the Sierra Nevada. In 1860, Otto Esche, a German-born San Francisco entrepreneur, imported fifteen two-humped bactrian camels from Asia. After a quick display of these "Ships of the Desert" for curious onlookers at San Francisco's German Benevolent Society, Esche's Camel Express went into business as commercial commodity transport to the Nevada mining regions. Esche hoped the express would flourish from San Francisco to Salt Lake City, and perhaps as far east as Missouri. The enterprise ultimately failed, but it gave us one of the most arresting images in Sierra Nevada history: a striking engraving in *Vischer's Views of California* shows an 1861 caravan of seven bactrian camels being escorted through the Calaveras Grove of Big Trees.

The Mammoth Grove Hotel, an 1862 engraving by Edward Vischer showing Otto Esche's Camel Express passing through the Calaveras Big Trees. Courtesy of The Bancroft Library, University of California, Berkeley, 1963.002:0385.o9–ALB.

THE FORGOTTEN VISIONARY

Theodore Judah

By the mid-nineteenth century, the United States had a serious case of railroad fever. Technological improvements and the development of successful railroad lines in the eastern states had proved this new mode of transport was both practical and profitable. A growing chorus called for construction of a transcontinental route that would expand American commercial prospects, provide tangible evidence of the nation's growing industrial might, and fulfill the dream of linking the country from sea to shining sea. The lingering question was the location of the route. Many possibilities were considered and surveys taken. Many championed northern roads through the plains or southern routes through the desert, and a few suggested a line through the northern Sierra Nevada.

Theodore Judah, c. 1860. Courtesy of The Bancroft Library, University of California, Berkeley; Judah, Theodore D.–POR 1.

Almost no one took seriously a route through the central Sierra Nevada, which would involve surmounting the imposingly steep eastern escarpment of the range, following the path of the tragic Donner Party. But one visionary believed in the central route: Theodore Judah.

In 1854, twenty-eight-year-old Judah came to California to build a railroad, having gained a reputation as an outstanding railroad man on projects back East, including building the Niagara Gorge Railroad. He had been hired by Charles Lincoln Wilson, president of the Sacramento Valley Railroad, to survey and construct a railroad line near Sacramento, and to everyone's surprise Judah confidently told Wilson that the route would ultimately extend over the Sierra Nevada.

Three years later, Judah visited the mountains, and in 1857 he published a pamphlet describing his idea of a Sierra Nevada route. The report, *A Practical Plan for Building a Pacific Railroad,* was a detailed prospectus and justification for his scheme. The introduction is a compelling and startlingly modern sales pitch:

> The project for construction of a great Railroad through the United States of America, connecting the Atlantic with the Pacific ocean, has been in agitation for over fifteen years.
>
> It is the most magnificent project ever conceived....
> It is a highway which leads to peace and future prosperity. An iron bond for the perpetuation of the Union and independence which we now enjoy....
>
> Yet—
>
> This project has not been consummated.
> The road has not been finished.
> Its practicability has not been established.
> A survey has not been made.
> It has simply been made the subject of reconnaissance.

Judah's wife Anna remarked to friends that the idea so dominated her husband's conversation that people were calling him "Pacific Railroad crazy." In 1889, Anna wrote a letter to researchers employed by prominent historian Hubert Howe Bancroft that echoed the sentiment:

Everything he did from the time he went to California to
the day of his death was for the great continental railway.
Time, money, brains, strength, body and soul were ab-
sorbed. It was the burden of his thought day and night,
largely of his conversation, till it used to be said "Judah's
Pacific Railroad crazy," and I would say, "Theodore, those
people don't care," or "you give your thunder away." He'd
laugh and say, "But we must keep the ball rolling."

Others felt that Judah was not only railroad crazy specifically but
just plain crazy. In 1925, in a letter to historian Carl Wheat, John McIntire of Sacramento recalled an 1861 or 1862 conversation with Newton
Booth, a Sacramento wholesale grocery merchant, McIntire's associ-
ate, and a future governor of California. When Booth saw Judah on
7th Street, he remarked to McIntire: "There comes Crazy Judah." Carl
Wheat described the reaction of John McIntire to Booth's comment:

Young McIntire had never seen an insane man, and was
therefore much interested, and since Judah's conversation with them seemed particularly sane and lucid, he
inquired the reason for Booth's remark, and was told that
Judah was a skilled engineer, but was so persistent in his
efforts in favor of a railroad across the mountains to con-
nect the eastern states that he had become almost mono-
maniac on the subject. Booth said he had been forced to
tell Judah not to approach him on the subject again.

Most observers felt that Booth's characterization of Crazy Judah was
apt, as few supposed a railroad line could be successfully constructed
over the great granite backbone of the central Sierra Nevada.

But Judah persisted. He spent many days and weeks in the range
searching for a potential route, and in time he came to believe he had
found his perfect path through the Sierra. After four more years and the
completion of several maps and a survey, Judah approached a prominent group of San Francisco investors. He was rebuffed but remained
undeterred, and soon he had convinced seven Sacramento investors to
back his Sierra Nevada railroad plan. The result was the Central Pacific Rail Road Company, incorporated in 1861. Four of the investors

became the company's officers: Leland Stanford was president (this well-known grocery merchant and budding politician would later serve California as both governor and US Senator); Collis P. Huntington, a hardware merchant, was selected as vice president; Mark Hopkins, Huntington's partner, was treasurer; and Charles Crocker, a dry goods merchant, headed the construction of the Central Pacific. Together they were known as the Big Four.

In late 1861, Judah lobbied Congress for funding for his planned route over the Sierra Nevada. Among the documents he presented was a comprehensive ninety-foot map of the proposed railroad showing eighteen tunnels and 140 miles of track. In July of the following year, Congress passed the Pacific Railroad Act, authorizing the construction of a transcontinental railroad, and Central Pacific was chosen to build the western end. Judah was delighted as he returned to Sacramento: "We have drawn the elephant, now let us see if we can harness him up."

As construction began in 1863, Judah became increasingly exasperated with the Big Four's attitudes and construction delays. In a letter to one of his earliest supporters, Dr. Daniel Strong of Dutch Flat, Judah was clearly frustrated: "I had a blow-out [with the board of directors] about two weeks ago and freed my mind, so much so that I looked for instant decapitation. I called things by their right name and invited war; but counsels of peace prevailed and my head is still on; [but] my hands are tied."

Judah decided to travel to New York to secure additional financing for the railroad that would allow him to buy out his infuriating partners. On November 2, 1863, he died suddenly of yellow fever, contracted while crossing the Isthmus of Panama. He was only thirty-seven years old. The Big Four completed the railroad and became some of the most famous—not to mention richest—men in America.

And what of Theodore Judah, the visionary of the entire enterprise? Although a few landmarks, streets, and schools are named for him, he is largely forgotten. His most visible monument is a commemorative marker tucked away on a seldom-visited side street in Old Sacramento, but of course his greatest legacy is the railroad running through the Sierra Nevada—a railroad built on the route Crazy Judah had envisioned and surveyed more than one hundred fifty years ago.

The Bloomer Cut

The Bloomer Cut, near Auburn, was one of the most dangerous construction locations on the entire Transcontinental Railroad line. The ground was composed of concreted aggregate that had to be removed with explosives. On April 15, 1864, one of the black powder charges failed to ignite, so two workers and the line's overall construction supervisor, James Strobridge, went in with tools—possibly crowbars—to remove the powder. When it exploded suddenly, all three were injured. One worker died a few days later, the second survived with just minor injuries, and Strobridge lost his left eye but, miraculously, returned to work the next day.

The dramatic and dangerous Bloomer Cut of the Central Pacific Railroad, near Auburn, Placer County. Photograph by Alfred A. Hart, c. 1870. From the series "Central Pacific Railroad, California, Scenes in the Sierra Nevada Mountains, c. 1865," No. 118, courtesy of the Library of Congress, Prints and Photographs Division, Washington, DC, LC-DIG-stereo-1s00565.

HALFWAY TO
THE STARS

Andrew Hallidie

Without doubt, one of the most recognizable civic symbols in the world is the San Francisco cable car, first made popular in the 1870s. The cable car's developer, Andrew Smith Hallidie, had an earlier claim to fame, though…in the Sierra Nevada.

Born in London in 1836, Andrew Smith was an inventor and engineer. He came from a long line of distinguished English subjects; his grandfather had fought at Waterloo, and his uncle, Sir Andrew Hallidie, had served as physician to King William IV and Queen Victoria. In fact, Andrew added the surname "Hallidie" in honor of his illustrious uncle.

In 1852, the teenaged Andrew Hallidie and his father left England for the goldfields of California. The pair tried gold mining to no avail, and the father gave up and returned to England just a few months later. Young Hallidie decided to stay, and for the next four years he struggled

Andrew Hallidie's Pine Street Bridge in Nevada City, Nevada County. This is believed to be the earliest photograph of the suspension bridge, c. 1866. Courtesy of The Bancroft Library, University of California, Berkeley, 1986.046–AX.

as a miner in various camps up and down the Mother Lode. From all accounts, he was a pathetic miner, but luckily he must have also been part cat, as he benefited from what seemed to be eight extra lives. Hallidie was almost buried by a mine cave-in; in Mokelumne Hill he was attacked by bandits; once he was caught in the middle of a forest fire; he barely escaped injury when a premature blast rocked a mine shaft he was exiting; he fell twenty-five feet from a suspension bridge; he slipped into rapids on the American River and survived a half-mile ride by clutching a floating piece of debris; and he was a passenger on a runaway stagecoach.

Having had enough of such adventures, Hallidie justifiably decided to find more sedate employment. During his mining days, he had experimented with "wire rope," or cable, as a means to transport ore cars, and that was where he turned his attention. In 1857, he entered into the wire rope manufacturing business, mostly supplying mines but also developing a reputation as a bridge builder. He used wire rope to suspend the bridges, just like today's Golden Gate Bridge. Starting in the early 1860s, he constructed bridges across the American River at Folsom, and he spanned the Bear, Trinity, Stanislaus, and Tuolumne Rivers. By 1867, he received a patent for his suspension bridge system.

In 1861, Nevada City contracted with the twenty-five-year-old Hallidie to erect a suspension bridge across Deer Creek. The $9,000 contract led to the construction of the Pine Street Bridge, which was completed in May 1862, although not without some controversy related to the then raging Civil War. Hallidie's practice was to place an American flag atop his creations when they neared completion, and Southern sympathizers who objected to Old Glory threatened vandalism or worse. When a crowd of angry onlookers started to gather near his latest structure, Hallidie grew concerned. He told his workers of the threats he had received and urged them to be on guard to protect the project. He also told his men that tar and feathers would be made available for use on the demonstrators if need be. Hallidie instructed them that a whistle would be the signal to respond, but the workers did not wait for the whistle. They immediately rushed to the bridge and the protestors hastily departed. The bridge was safe…or so it appeared.

Just two months after its dedication, the Pine Street Bridge collapsed. Under the weight of a twenty-oxen team driven by four men, an anchor bolt failed, and the bridge fell sixty feet to the creek bed below. Fifteen oxen and two men died.

Hallidie quickly set to work repairing the damage, and several months later, with thousands of dollars of additional cost, the bridge was reopened in November 1862. Despite initial misgivings by the public about its safety, the Pine Street Bridge would remain in service, problem-free, for another forty years before its suspension system was replaced with truss arches.

With the discovery of silver in the Comstock Lode in the 1860s, wire rope was in even greater demand in the mines. Hallidie gave up bridge construction and devoted himself exclusively to wire cable manufacturing at his factory headquarters in San Francisco.

He also continued to experiment. Hallidie developed a patent for what he called the "Hallidie Ropeway," a means of transporting ore and other materials by using an endless, elevated, continuously moving wire cable. Today we would call it a tramway, and it works on the same principle as a ski lift.

In 1871, Hallidie completed plans for his newest invention: a system by which San Francisco streetcars could be propelled by underground wire ropes. The cars would use a connecting apparatus called a "grip" to attach to and detach from the constantly rotating loops of cable below the street, a perfect solution for the hilly city. By 1873, with sufficient capital raised and equipment built and at the ready, Andrew Hallidie's cable cars—later admired in song as climbing "halfway to the stars"—sprang to life. And the rest is history.

The Emerald Bay Bridge

Sometimes the bridge that isn't built is as influential as the one that is. In the late 1950s, the California Division of Highways recommended a multilane freeway on the west shore of Lake Tahoe to replace the winding and dangerous two-lane road. The state (and commercial interests like the Lake Tahoe Chamber of Commerce) argued that the new roadway would enrich the business climate, enhance safety, increase convenience, and even improve the view. There was an immediate public outcry. West shore residents decried the likely degradation of the scenery, the disruption of the rural amenities that had drawn them to Lake Tahoe in the first place, and, most importantly, the inconceivable construction of a proposed bridge at picturesque Emerald Bay, the jewel of Lake Tahoe. Some outraged inhabitants organized nonprofit protest groups, among which was the Tahoe Improvement and Conservation Association, later renamed the League to Save Lake Tahoe. Their "Keep Tahoe Blue" logo has become a regional environmental icon that persists to this day. Uproar over the freeway proposal and other suggested developments soon led to the establishment of the Tahoe Regional Planning Agency, which regulates growth in the Lake Tahoe Basin and helps preserve its natural wonder. The Emerald Bay Bridge never moved beyond the planning stage.

III - ED - 38 - B
Plate B

A rendering of the proposed Emerald Bay Bridge at Lake Tahoe, published by the California Department of Highways, 1960. *Emerald Bay Route Studies, State Legislative Route 36, November 1960*, California Division of Highways, III–ED-38-B, Plate B, courtesy of the Government Publications Collection, California State Library, Sacramento, P2200 E5b.

HIDDEN HISTORY

African Americans in the Sierra Nevada

African Americans were rare in the Sierra Nevada, even in the days when all types of people were coming from all over the world in hopes of striking it rich. The census of 1850 showed that the entire state of California was home to only about 100 black people that year, although the number rose dramatically—to around 2,500 blacks, including 90 women, in 1852—as word spread that no other place in the United States offered a quicker road to freedom for slaves than California. Frederick Douglass, the prominent black abolitionist leader, even urged the American Colonization Society to abandon its idea of repatriating newly freed slaves to Africa and instead resettle them in California.

One of the earliest and most prominent African Americans in the Sierra Nevada was James Beckwourth. The son of a Revolutionary War officer and his slave mistress, Beckwourth left his Southern

Painting of William Alexander Leidesdorff, prominent early California African American land baron and entrepreneur, c. 1845. Courtesy of The Bancroft Library, University of California, Berkeley, 1956.014–CASE.

home to become a Western mountain man in the 1820s. Well known for his creative storytelling, he claimed he was captured by Crow Indians in 1826 and marked for death, but through his charm and guile, he saved himself, having convinced the Indians he was actually the son of a Crow chief and had been kidnapped as a child by the Cheyenne. The ruse worked and Beckwourth not only escaped execution but was taken in to the Crow tribe, married a chief's daughter, and eventually became chief himself just a few years later. When the Gold Rush hit, James Beckwourth seized his opportunity and made his name in various ventures, including establishing trading posts and a settlement (the town of Beckwourth), improving a mountain path for travelers (Beckwourth Trail), and reportedly discovering a more convenient, low-elevation pass in the northern Sierra (Beckwourth Pass).

But Beckwourth was a notable exception: in the first blush of the Gold Rush, there were almost no African Americans in the region. One obvious reason was the persistent institution of slavery. By California law at the time, it cost $1,000 to buy a slave's freedom—an amount equal to about four years of average income. It was not an inconsiderable sum by any means, but in the freewheeling economy of the Gold Rush, that kind of cash could be realized with greater ease. In one case, a slave in California was allowed to keep part of the profits from a laundry his master ran in San Francisco. As the city boomed, so did the business proceeds, and the slave was able to purchase his freedom in only five weeks. There were similar stories throughout the Sierra Nevada, for despite the pervasive and often dangerous bigotry that most African Americans faced daily in the region, there was a slim avenue of opportunity.

Consider the case of Alvin Coffey, a slave who came to Sacramento from Missouri in 1849 with his master, known as Mr. Duvall. Over the next eight months, Coffey worked in the mines and earned his master $5,000, while also picking up extra work—mining under a separate contract and washing clothes for other miners—thereby earning an additional $700 of his own. Duvall had arrived in Gold Country physically ill and there grew progressively worse until he eventually returned to Missouri with Coffey, whom he then sold to Nelson Tindle. Tindle told Coffey he was too smart to be a slave and urged him to purchase his own freedom. Coffey, who longed to return to California, informed Tindle that if permitted to revisit the Golden State, he could easily earn enough money to buy his freedom. Tindle agreed to the plan, and within a few weeks of their arrival in California, Coffey had earned $1,500 and was a free man. He then earned enough funds to purchase the freedom of his wife and daughters, who were slaves of a Dr. Basset in Missouri. The family was reunited in California. In all, Coffey had earned more than $7,000 to gain his and his family's freedom, an amount that would today total almost $200,000.

Several slaveholding forty-niners failed as miners and, needing funds to return to their homes, they sometimes sold their slaves. In one instance, Caleb Fay, an ardent abolitionist, responded to an advertisement in a San Francisco newspaper, purchased the slave for $1,000, and promptly granted freedom to the young man.

Many African Americans improved their fortunes, both literal and figurative, in the wake of the Gold Rush, but one in particular came to the state *before* the frenzy and prospered, to say the least. His name was William Alexander Leidesdorff, the son of a Danish father and a black Caribbean mother. He arrived in San Francisco in 1841, when the little hamlet was still known as Yerba Buena, and almost immediately, he excelled in business. He built San Francisco's first hotel, constructed its first public school, owned the state's first steamship, and even conducted California's first horse race. He operated out of lavish headquarters—the Leidesdorff Building—one of the finest structures in the city.

In 1844, Leidesdorff acquired a 35,000-acre grant in the interior of Northern California called Rancho Rios de los Americanos. When Leidesdorff died in 1848, at age thirty-six, Joseph Folsom purchased the property for $75,000, but Leidesdorff's family felt the estate had been swindled and they sued Joseph Folsom in 1850. The case was dismissed because blacks were not allowed to testify in court against whites, and Joseph Folsom kept the land, ultimately giving his name to the city of Folsom, located within the boundaries of the old Rancho Rios de los Americanos. Today, the only lasting vestige of Leidesdorff's legacy is a sign that designates the stretch of Highway 50 that passes through Folsom as the William Alexander Leidesdorff Memorial Highway.

Charles Young and the Buffalo Soldiers

Before the National Park Service was established in 1916, the United States Army oversaw the national parks for thirty years. Yosemite and Sequoia National Parks were notably manned by the Buffalo Soldiers, the highly decorated African American units of the 9th Cavalry and 24th Mounted Infantry. One of their commanders was Charles Young of the 9th Cavalry. Young was the third black graduate of West Point and had served in the Spanish American War in Cuba, helping rescue Teddy Roosevelt during the Battle of San Juan Hill. Young became the superintendent of Sequoia National Park in 1903 and later served as a military attaché to embassies in Haiti and Liberia. In 2013, the Obama administration announced the establishment of a new national monument in Ohio to honor the Buffalo Soldiers: the Charles Young Buffalo Soldiers National Monument.

US Army colonel, Buffalo Soldier, and superintendent of Sequoia National Park Charles Young, pictured as a lieutenant soon after graduation from West Point, c. 1890. Courtesy of the Ohio Historical Society, Columbus, Ohio, NAAMCC: NAM_MSS3_B02F50.01.tiff.

204. Heading of east portal Tunnel No. 8.

DAWN AND DARKNESS

Gold Mountain and the Chinese

The history of Chinese people in the Sierra Nevada region is inexorably linked to the Gold Rush. As soon as the 1848 discovery was announced in China, many yearned to visit "Gam Saan"—Gold Mountain—as the Chinese called California. It was a fabled land bursting with hope and unimaginable wealth. In an 1848 letter translated and published in Boston, a Cantonese man wrote to his brother: "Good many Americans speak of California. Oh! Very rich country!...Oh! They find gold very quickly, so I hear....I feel as if I should go there very much. I think I shall go to California next summer."

Chinese people had been a presence in the state for many years, but during and following the Gold Rush, the numbers increased dramatically. Census figures predating 1850, when California was granted

A Chinese Central Pacific Railroad worker at the entrance to a tunnel near Donner Summit. Photograph by Alfred A. Hart, c. 1865. From the series "Central Pacific Railroad, California, Scenes in the Sierra Nevada Mountains, c. 1865," no. 204, courtesy of the Library of Congress, Prints and Photographs Division, Washington, DC, LC-DIG-stereo-1s00553.

statehood, are questionable, but the numbers indicate that from 1840 to 1850 approximately 400 Chinese immigrants came to California. From 1850 to 1855, during the zenith of the Gold Rush, the number topped 27,000.

The vast majority of Chinese immigrants were male. They referred to themselves as "Gam Saan Haak"—Travelers to Gold Mountain—and considered themselves not settlers but temporary visitors hoping to get rich quick in the goldfields and return to their homeland. Females of any race were rare in the Sierra Nevada during the period, but Chinese women were especially scarce. Of those 27,000 Chinese immigrants who arrived between 1850 and 1855, only 675 were women, and the difference became even more pronounced during the construction of the Transcontinental Railroad in the 1860s; in 1862, Chinese immigrants totaled 7,214, of whom only one was female. It was not until the post–World War II era that female Chinese immigrants outnumbered males.

Most of the newcomers gravitated to the mining areas, where the Chinese populations were significant—18 percent of the overall population of Sierra Nevada counties, according to the census of 1860. In some specific areas, the concentration was even higher: Placer County was 22 percent Chinese, Amador County was 23.5 percent, and Mariposa County was 30 percent.

Chinese settlements were overwhelmingly "bachelor" communities, populated by a combination of unmarried men and husbands separated from their families in China. Strangers in a strange land, they were often lonely and apprehensive, and they clustered for support and protection. As Geling Yan, a modern Chinese novelist, put it: "They of course clung together in groups, like cans of sardines shipped from China. They were bony and small....They sensed that there would be danger, and that they must stick together." They sought release in the usual vices of men thrust together in hard times, including gambling, drinking, and fighting. Not trusting local authorities to protect them, many Gam Saan Haak bought weapons for self-defense and community security; knives, rifles, and revolvers were not uncommon.

Their stores were like those back home: wide-open storefronts with groceries and vegetables overflowing onto the sidewalks. They served as communication hubs and social centers, as one migrant recalled:

> All Chinese came. Not just relatives. They all like just to get together...Sometimes they even get some idea from China....[T]hey send a letter over here, we get together and talk it over—and send it back. We communicate, see, otherwise you're alone. You know nothing.

The settlements were temporary but fully functional. They had newspapers, barbers, doctors, herbalists, and assayers. There were boarding houses, temples, theaters, and cemeteries. Some Chinatowns were honeycombed with interconnecting tunnels used for storage, icehouses, secret meetings, and escape routes. Through it all, the Chinese preserved their cultural identity while adjusting to the new land.

These early Chinese immigrants helped transform the Sierra Nevada from a rugged landscape into a more livable community. Chinese men built many roads, railroads, and other important elements of the infrastructure, including the Big Gap Flume in Mariposa County in the 1850s. By 1852, the Chinese were leaders in land improvement projects, and were even praised by California governor John McDougal for swamp and flooded lands reclamation. Chinese immigrants were pioneer workers in the wine industry and were the only farmers who could successfully cultivate celery in the area. Much of the region's fruit industry depended upon Chinese labor.

But despite their significant contributions, the Chinese often found themselves facing difficult, if not impossible, circumstances. By law, the Chinese did not have citizenship rights and therefore could not vote, own property, or file mining claims, yet they were required to pay taxes. Chinese people could not testify in court against whites and were the frequent targets of racial attacks. In 1850, the California State Legislature passed the Foreign Miners Tax, which required "foreign miners" to purchase a license for twenty dollars month, but the measure was quickly amended to exempt white miners and anyone who could become an American citizen. The law, primarily targeted at Spanish-speaking and Chinese miners, raised nearly $5 million between 1854 and 1870, 98 percent of which was paid by Chinese miners.

Some Chinese immigrants reported warm welcomes upon reaching the golden shores of California—in 1855, San Francisco merchant Lai Chu-Chuen remarked, "The people of the flowery land were received like guests [and] greeted with favor....From far and near we came and were pleased"—but almost immediately upon arrival in the mining regions, the Chinese faced discrimination. As early as 1852, Yuba County passed a resolution requiring all Chinese to leave. Soon afterward, the Columbia Mining District officially banned "Asiatics and South Sea Islanders" from holding mining claims. As more Chinese arrived, the legal and physical violence intensified.

To combat the ongoing hostility, and to aid new immigrants adjusting to the unfamiliar culture, the Chinese organized voluntary associations for assistance and protection. These groups were benevolent, fraternal, and mutual aid societies, similar to village councils in China. The central "company house" kept a register of names and addresses and they were often wrongly accused of working with other Chinese groups that ran criminal enterprises, such as prostitution rings.

Nevertheless, Chinese immigrants kept coming to California, and during the 1860s, they were the most important laborers in the construction of the Transcontinental Railroad over the Sierra Nevada. An estimated 90 percent of the workforce on the western leg of the line was Chinese. For generations, little was known of the anonymous thousands who had built the grandest civil engineering project of the nineteenth century, but recent scholarship has filled in some of the blanks, uncovered names and personal details. We now know that in 1864, Hung Wah and Ah Toy were the first of approximately ten thousand Chinese immigrants hired to work on the historic rail line.

Racial discrimination was as prevalent on the job as it was anywhere else. Chinese laborers were paid thirty dollars monthly while white laborers were paid thirty-five dollars. The Chinese had to provide their own food while the white workers did not. The Chinese tended to be healthier than their white counterparts due to frequent sponge baths, to a more nutritionally balanced diet, and for their broad refusal to drink potentially contaminated groundwater. The Chinese laborers drank freshly brewed tea that was available at the construction grade.

One of the most persistent legends about the Chinese in the history of the American West took place just east of Colfax in Placer County, where the railroad right-of-way enters a rocky precipice called Cape Horn. In 1865, Chinese workers carved the roadbed out of the outcropping, and reports from the time indicated that the workers were dangled over the sheer, stony ledge in wicker baskets to prepare the route with sledges, hand drills, and black powder. According to these accounts, the workers set the explosive fuses and were lifted out of danger just before the detonations. This story is highly dramatic, widely cited, and utterly false; studies conducted by historians and engineers have revealed that the tale of the building of Cape Horn was journalistic exaggeration at best and, more likely, a company's publicity stunt. This debunking does not, however, diminish the heroic efforts of the Chinese workers, who blasted tunnels into seemingly impenetrable Sierra granite and constructed, without any mortar, the towering stone railroad trestle at Donner Summit—a spectacular edifice called the "China Wall."

There were numerous labor and management disputes between the Central Pacific leadership and its immigrant workforce—even a strike—but in the end, the Chinese were valued for their skill and work ethic. In October 1865, Leland Stanford, president of the Central Pacific, reported to US President Andrew Johnson that "the greater portion of the laborers employed by us are Chinese, who constitute a large element in the population of California. Without them it would be impossible to complete the western portion of this great national enterprise....As a class they are quiet, peaceable, patient, industrious and economical—ready and apt to learn all the different kinds of work required in railroad building."

On May 10, 1869, the eastern and western portions of the Transcontinental Railroad were linked with a ceremony at Promontory Summit in Utah, with prominent figures from the two railroad companies—the Union Pacific and Central Pacific—in attendance. The honor of laying the final Central Pacific tracks was given to eight Chinese laborers, and following the ceremony, James Strobridge, the Central Pacific's construction superintendent, invited other Chinese laborers to dine with him and his special guests in his private coach. As the *San Francisco Newsletter*

reported, "When [the Chinese workers] entered, all the guests and officers present cheered them as the chosen representatives of the race which
have greatly helped to build the road...[,] a tribute they well deserved
and which evidently gave them much pleasure." Strobridge is believed
to have individually recognized Hung Wah, the first and longest-serving
Chinese employee on the project. In 1919, three of the surviving Chinese
laborers—Ging Cui, Wong Fook, and Lee Shao—were guests of honor at
the railroad's fiftieth anniversary celebration in Ogden, Utah.

The following statement, made by Central Pacific Railroad official
Edwin B. Crocker at a celebration of the railroad's completion, illus-
trates the complicated status of Chinese immigrants in America: "I wish
to call to your minds that the early completion of this railroad we have
built has been in a large measure to that poor, despised class of laborers called the Chinese, to the fidelity and industry they have shown."
Unfortunately, "fidelity and industry" did not translate into respect, and
bigotry against the Chinese not only persisted but increased as they
tried to find work after the railroad project ended in 1869.

Chinatowns became more common as many cities forced immigrants to live on the outskirts of town, if not completely outside city
limits, and Chinese workers were routinely denied jobs in positions
outside of agriculture, laundry, restaurants, and domestic help. They
were increasingly victimized by a virulent anti-Chinese movement,
which included countless assaults on their communities and numerous discriminatory ordinances. The Cubic Air Ordinance of 1871, a
cynical reworking of a New York anti-tenement law, regulated the size
of living and working quarters; in Sonora, the city arrested hundreds
of Chinese immigrants claimed to be in violation because they lived in
cramped housing. Residence requirements often forced the Chinese to
settle on undesirable land or build along riverbeds prone to flooding.
San Francisco's Sidewalk Ordinance of 1870 prohibited the use of poles
to carry bundles, a traditional Chinese activity, and the city's Queue
Ordinance required jailed Chinese immigrants to cut their long braids,
even though a queue was mandatory for their return to China under
the Qing dynasty. Various laundry ordinances were in effect as well,
including those collecting higher taxes from Chinese owners and those

restricting the kinds of buildings that could house laundries. One law forbade laundries in wooden buildings during the time when virtually every building was made of wood. Schools and cemeteries were segregated. Interracial marriage was prohibited. Laws were passed to make it almost impossible for Chinese people to attend school, to work, and to find suitable housing.

At the same time, an economic depression devastated California. Unemployment was high, projected economic benefits from the railroad did not materialize, and the state's fledgling manufacturing industry suffered in competition with cheaply made goods from the East Coast. The Chinese were blamed for the downturn, although in reality the opposite was true: the Chinese had contributed tremendously to the economic development of California through railroad construction and land reclamation, and an 1877 congressional report concluded that a $290 million increase in state property values was due in large part to Chinese labor.

Regardless, Chinese immigrants were targeted as scapegoats, and violence against them escalated. In the 1870s, 20 percent of the workforce in California's Butte County was Chinese, and as the economy faltered there, anti-Chinese backlash intensified. Butte County's Chinese miners were already denied access to the goldfields and legally barred from holding claims, and unemployed white workers marched in torchlight parades carrying banners reading "The Yellow Devils Must Go!" In 1876, the town of Chico organized the Supreme Order of the Caucasians, which issued a list of "public enemies" that included anyone who replaced a white employee with a Chinese worker; retained a Chinese nurse; defended Chinese against whites in court; employed a Chinese worker in any "saloons, coffee houses, cigar stores, [or] restaurants"; rented property to Chinese; or published a newspaper that advocated "the presence of Mongolians in America." The society grew to more than two hundred members and included, the *Chico Butte Record* reported, "some of our best citizens." In the months that followed, the Order resorted to arson, gunfights, threats of assassination, and murder. When the town's founder, John Bidwell—a politician, land baron, and the largest employer of Chinese workers in California—publicly protested on the grounds that much of the region's wealth was owed to the immigrants' labor, one of his barns was torched before a cheering crowd.

In September 1877, anti-Chinese brutality engulfed the railroad town of Rocklin, some twenty miles east of Sacramento and at one time the western terminus of the Transcontinental Railroad. The bodies of two murdered white men were found on a ranch a few hundred yards from the Chinese farming ground known as China Gardens, on the outskirts of Rocklin, and a third victim, barely alive, identified the assailants as Chinese before dying of his wounds later that night. Following the "traces of Chinese shoes" and other flimsy evidence, the police arrested ten Chinese men at China Gardens. A lynch mob gathered.

The following day, the mob informed the four hundred Chinese residents of Rocklin that they had to depart by 6 p.m. that day. If they did not leave, "those that remained would be driven out." By 4 p.m., the Chinese had left and an angry rabble descended on the deserted Chinese Quarter. Twenty-five houses were demolished with axes before the entire settlement was set ablaze, every shop and house destroyed.

Fearing for the safety of the Chinese men he had arrested, the county sheriff attempted to move them to the Placer County Jail in Auburn, about ten miles east. As the train began to pull out of Rocklin, the lynch mob rushed the train yelling, "Hang them! Hang them!" Deputies forcibly removed the vigilantes from the train and the Chinese were safely transferred. The sheriff later concluded that the Chinese were most likely not the perpetrators and released them.

The murderers were never found, and the damage had been done. Over the next few days, the nearby communities of Penryn, Loomis, and Roseville issued orders for their Chinese residents to leave immediately, and in the coming weeks, Chinese "purges" spread from the Sacramento Delta to the crest of the Sierra Nevada. The Chinese community never returned to Rocklin, and in 1879, civic boosters declared that "no Chinaman can rent a house or obtain employment in the town." In 1882, the admired, widely disseminated *Thompson and West's History of Placer County* proudly proclaimed, "Not a Chinaman is to be found in Rocklin."

SIERRA SPOTLIGHT

Yee Fung Cheung and the Chew Kee Store

Chinese herbal remedies were remarkably sophisticated in comparison to Western medicines available in the mid-nineteenth century. Even now, many of today's "wonder drugs" are scientifically synthesized versions of Chinese herbal preparations that have been around for hundreds of years. The Sierra Nevada village of Fiddletown, in Amador County, has its own connection to the Chinese medical legacy in the form of the Chew Kee Store, built about 1850.

Among the Chinese immigrants who came to the region during the first years of the Gold Rush was Yee Fung Cheung, the young son of a prominent family. He grew up to become Dr. Yee Fung Cheung, a talented and respected herbalist who established stores in Fiddletown, Sacramento, and Virginia City. In 1880, Dr. Yee Fung Cheung hired Chew Kee as an assistant in Fiddletown, and by the 1890s, Chew Kee owned the Fiddletown store and his name was thereafter applied to the business.

In 1862, Dr. Yee Fung Cheung provided an herbal remedy that relieved the severe pulmonary distress of Jane Lathrop Stanford, the wife of California governor Leland Stanford. Yee Fung Cheung died in 1907, but his memory remains through the fully restored Chew Kee Store, rightfully included in the National Register of Historic Places.

The Chew Kee Store, a Gold Rush–era Chinese herbal medicine dispensary in Fiddletown, Amador County. Photograph by Alma Lavenson, 1946. Courtesy of The Bancroft Library, University of California, Berkeley, 1987.021:149–PIC.

The Heathen Chinee

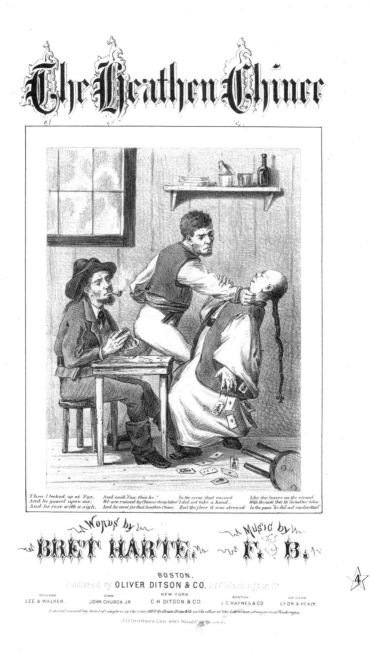

Then I looked up at Nye,   And said, "Can this be?   In the scene that ensued   Like the leaves on the strand
And he gazed upon me;   We are ruined by Chinese cheap labor." I did not take a hand,   With the cards that Ah Sin had been hiding,
And he rose with a sigh.   And he went for that heathen Chinee.   But the floor it was strewed   In the game "he did not understand."

Words by
BRET HARTE.

Music by
F. B.

BOSTON.
Published by OLIVER DITSON & CO. 277 Washington St.

PHILAD.A   CINN.   NEW YORK.   BOSTON   CHICAGO
LEE & WALKER.   JOHN CHURCH JR.   C.H DITSON & CO.   J C HAYNES & CO   LYON & HEALY

Entered according to act of congress in the year 1870 by Oliver Ditson & Co. in the office of The Librarian of congress at Washington.

J.H.Bufford's Lith 490 Wash'n St Boston

INSTRUMENTS
OF DARKNESS
The Chinese Exclusion Act of 1882

Just outside Auburn, in Placer County, is a two-acre plot along-side Highway 49 that's easy to miss. Bracketing the entrance are two weather-beaten wooden posts with a warping plank spanning the crown. Decorated simply with hand-painted white letters, it reads "Chinese Cemetery." The graveyard dates back to the Gold Rush and is now overgrown with irregularly spaced oak trees, native grasses, and star thistle. With care, one can navigate a slender path through the weeds and see several headstones adorned with Chinese characters poking through the vegetation. There is also a foot-tall historical marker with a fading metal plaque, and a head-high, three-foot-square brick structure with a pyramidal cap and a round chimney called a funerary burner, which was used to burn ceremonial tributes—such as paper or cardboard facsimiles of money, clothing, or houses—meant to assist

Cover sheet for a musical version of Bret Harte's poem "The Heathen Chinee," 1870. While Harte intended his verse as satire, anti-Chinese advocates considered "The Heathen Chinee" a publication that supported their cause. Courtesy of The Bancroft Library, University of California, Berkeley, xffF870.M9.C6 No. 59.

the deceased in the afterlife. Nearly everywhere you look, everywhere you step, there are two-foot-deep, coffin-sized depressions marking where bodies have been disinterred, either to be returned to China or reburied in other nearby cemeteries. In the past, this hallowed ground had dozens of gravesites, but now only eleven remain.

In 1882, the United States Congress passed the Chinese Exclusion Act, legislation cosponsored and strongly supported by California senator Aaron Sargent, a resident of Nevada City. The law excluded Chinese laborers, skilled or unskilled, from entering the country for ten years. A few narrowly defined professionals and merchants were allowed in, but often even highly respected members of the Chinese community, such as herbalists, were categorized as laborers and prohibited from immigrating. Merchants could arrange for their wives to join them, but laborers could not. Over night, Chinese American workers were forced to decide whether to stay in the United States or return to China.

Immigration and population patterns changed dramatically in response to the Exclusion Act. In 1882, just prior to its passage, Census Bureau documents indicate that 39,579 Chinese people immigrated to the United States, including 116 women. In 1887, the total number of Chinese immigrants to the United States was ten.

The Chinese population in Sierra Nevada counties also plummeted precipitously. From 1880 to 1900, the overall percentage of Chinese residents in the Sierra Nevada region declined by 43 percent. In some counties, like El Dorado and Calaveras, the decline was as much as 86 percent.

Although the overall population of Chinese immigrants decreased, the number of incidents of discrimination and violence against those who remained jumped appreciably during this time. Reported incidents of physical and work violence, job discrimination, demonstrations and rallies, murder, mayhem, and prejudicial governmental actions directed against the Chinese in California numbered in the hundreds in the decade following the passage of the Exclusion Act. Article XIX of the 1879 California constitution made it illegal for corporations to hire Chinese workers and provided legal cover for towns expelling Chinese residents, among which was Nevada City, whose trustees in 1880 ordered all Chinese to leave within sixty days. In 1880, the California legislature passed an anti-miscegenation bill that was incorporated into the civil law code. Chinese businesses were boycotted, and city leaders passed restrictive laundry ordinances that often forced the sale of Chinese property. California governor George C. Perkins declared March 4, 1880, as a legal holiday for anti-Chinese demonstrations, and anti-Chinese parades and rallies were not uncommon at any time of year. The Southern Pacific Railroad forced Chinese laborers to work in pools of volatile oil—thirty-one workers died as a result—and in Auburn, along the Transcontinental Railroad line that Chinese workers had built, the Chinatown was burned to the ground. Coloma, where James Marshall first discovered gold, celebrated the construction of the first local railroad line that did *not* use Chinese labor.

Chinese people were beaten and murdered and also imprisoned—often on dubious charges—at a higher rate; Chinese immigrants made up roughly 7 percent of California's population, but they accounted for 20 percent of the state's prisoners. In Truckee in 1885, the town began a starvation campaign against the Chinese, a horrifying technique that became infamous as the "Truckee Method." In the mining camp of Bloomfield, the town well was poisoned, for which the Chinese were blamed and forcibly removed. The community of Latrobe publicly declared that it would boycott all the Chinese in their town, despite the fact that no Chinese lived in Latrobe. Near Marysville, Chinese hop pruners were assaulted and their houses burned. In Sonora, an anti-Chinese club secretly purchased arms and raided Chinese homes.

The Chinese, along with supporters who refused to obey these racist policies, did not meekly submit to these outrages. In 1882 in Amador City, Chinese residents countered hostilities by forming an armed militia fifty strong. In Dutch Flat in 1883, Chinese workers refused to leave town despite threats and arson. In Nevada City, the sizeable Chinese population reinforced their dwellings with bars, bolts, and other "fastenings," and in Truckee in 1885, in response to the "Truckee Method," local Chinese ordered Winchester rifles, muskets, and cartridges from San Francisco in self-defense. In Wheatland, Chinese gardeners took a gentler approach and simply undercut the white competition by selling vegetables at a 25 percent discount.

Local governments also started coming around. In Sonora, despite howling protests from the public, the city ordered the Tuolumne County Hospital to admit a Chinese patient. In Grass Valley and Quincy, the city government refused to endorse a Chinese boycott. In San Francisco, the courts ruled that most discriminatory legislation targeting Chinese was unconstitutional.

In this litany of darkness, there were moments of mutual trust and tolerance, as demonstrated by the story of Yee Ah Tye of LaPorte.

Yee Ah Tye was born in the Sze Yup region of southern China's Guangdong Province and immigrated to California in 1852, at the age of twenty-nine. He spent his first night in San Francisco huddled in a building doorway. Educated in Hong Kong, Yee spoke English and soon became a conduit between Chinese immigrants and the white community. He became a leader of the Sze Yup District Association and, as the *San Francisco Herald* reported in 1853, succeeded "by his superior adroitness, influence and cunning."

Wishing to be closer to the goldfields, in 1854 Yee relocated to Sacramento, where he continued to cultivate good relations with the white business community. In 1861, in a widely reported incident, Yee hosted a handful of white men—a judge, a physician, a lawyer, two newspaper reporters, and other prominent leaders—at a Chinese New Year celebration. In the 1860s, he moved to the boomtown of LaPorte, the hub of rich diggings in Plumas and Sierra Counties, which at the time had 1,000 residents, of which 136 were Chinese. (As of 2010, LaPorte has a population of 26.) Yee became a partner and later president of the Hop Sing and Company Store, which sold goods to the general populace and also contracted Chinese laborers, and as his store prospered through the 1870s, he used the profits to build Chinese boarding houses and invest in mining claims in Nevada and Sierra Counties. Now married with four children, he was well known and respected by Chinese and whites alike.

And then came the Chinese Exclusion Act.

Following the lead of other Sierra Nevada communities, LaPorte formed an Anti-Chinese League and called for the expulsion of the immigrants in their midst. Tellingly, however, the local league called for peaceable actions only and, as the organization's manifesto stated, "We imperatively discountenance any unlawful means of ridding ourselves of the Chinese." While other towns were destroying Chinatowns and forcibly expelling immigrants en masse, LaPorte adopted a halfhearted boycott that was largely due to peer pressure and mostly affected the mines.

Concerned for his children's education and safety, Yee returned them to China, while he stayed on with Hop Sing and Company, which continued to operate profitably under a multiethnic partnership that was unheard of at the time. Yee was the proprietor and Frenchman Frank Cayot, the owner of the LaPorte Union Hotel, was the bookkeeper. The company's partners included Chinese merchants and miners Ah Wah, Ah Fook, Ah Chuck, Ah Sing, Ah Chung, and Ah Sam, and local businessmen Henry Buckley from Ireland, Charles Pike from New York, Frank Steward from Maine, Dixon Brabban from England, and Yee's long-time business partner, Charles Hendel from Germany. Most believed that Yee's enduring friendships with this diverse group of neighbors allowed Hop Sing and Company to weather the worst of the exclusion storm. The records of the Plumas County Tax Assessor show that Yee's firm was one of the largest taxpayers in the county at the time.

Yee Ah Tye died in 1896. He had lived in LaPorte for more than twenty years and was widely admired for his honesty and generosity. The *Downieville Mountain Messenger* described him as "wealthy and liberal to a fault." The *Plumas National-Bulletin* eulogized him as well:

> He was a Chinese of unusual intelligence and business capacity, and a courteous gentlemen. He leaves quite a family, all of the children being good English scholars, and the girls accomplished musicians. They have many friends among the Americans who will feel sorry for their bereavement.

Most Chinese immigrants to America left instructions to have their bones shipped back to China for burial on ancestral land so their spirits would not forever wander in a foreign world. But Yee Ah Tye astounded his family and friends with his dying request: since he had lived nearly fifty years in America and never returned to China, he said, "Now let my body be buried here and my bones lie undisturbed for all times in the land where I have lived."

Restrictions against Chinese and other immigrants continued for decades. In 1892, passage of the Geary Act renewed the Exclusion Act for ten additional years. The Exclusion Act was renewed again in 1902, and then extended indefinitely in 1904. Twenty years later, with minimal opposition, the federal Asian Exclusion Act denied admission to any immigrant "ineligible for citizenship"—the primary targets being the Chinese and Japanese. The legislation was part of the package known as the Immigration Act of 1924, which established a formula of annual quotas on immigration from all countries.

In 1943, President Franklin D. Roosevelt signed the "Act to Repeal the Chinese Exclusion Acts, to Establish Quotas, and for Other Purposes." This measure repealed all the versions of the Chinese Exclusion Act and allowed an annual immigration quota of about 105 Chinese. The law was the result of wartime exigencies, since the Republic of China was an American ally during World War II and the repeal was made as a gesture of goodwill. Federal exclusion of Asian immigrants was finally ended with the Immigration Act of 1952, although the quota system for all immigrants was not abolished until the passage of the Immigration Act of 1965.

SIERRA SPOTLIGHT

The Truckee Method

The passage of the Chinese Exclusion Act of 1882 prompted an increase in anti-Chinese violence in the Sierra Nevada. Some Sierra communities advocated the brutal "Tacoma Method" of Chinese removal, which was essentially barbaric mob violence with the intent to destroy lives and property. In the mid-1880s, one Sierra town proposed their supposedly kinder and gentler solution.

Encouraged by Charles McGlashan, a prominent Truckee businessman, newspaper publisher, and chronicler of the Donner Party, the

"Truckee Method" was basically a citywide boycott that led to the starvation of its Chinese residents. In 1885, McGlashan formed the Truckee Anti-Chinese Boycotting Committee; the group pledged to refuse service of all kinds to any Chinese person in Truckee. Their boycott began in earnest in 1886, and within weeks, they had driven most of the 1,500 Chinese from town. Four months after the boycott started, a massive fire destroyed Truckee's Chinatown and killed several inhabitants. City officials claimed the Chinese had set the fire themselves. The remaining handful of Chinese people then left the town, and the white residents declared their technique a success. Charles McGlashan proudly embarked on a speaking tour to promote the infamous Truckee Method.

A view of Truckee from the Rocking Stone. This Sierra Nevada railroad town originated an infamous anti-Chinese tactic known as "The Truckee Method" in the 1880s. Photograph by Henry Kimball Gage, c. 1880. From the California History Room Picture Collection: Nevada County: Truckee, no. 2008-1675, courtesy of the California State Library, Sacramento.

A. A. Sargent

POWER COUPLE

The Sargents

In the 1872 presidential election, activist Susan B. Anthony cast her vote for Ulysses S. Grant. A few days later, she was issued an arrest warrant charging her with voting in a federal election "without having a lawful right to vote." Since women's suffrage in national elections was illegal at the time, Anthony was tried, convicted (after being refused the right to testify), and fined one hundred dollars, which she refused to pay. It was a seminal moment in the struggle for women's voting rights.

It remained illegal for women to vote in presidential elections until 1920, forty-eight years after Anthony's initial attempt. In August of that year, the Nineteenth Amendment to the United States Constitution was

Ellen Clark Sargent, a leading California suffragist in the late nineteenth and early twentieth century, c. 1900. From *How We Won the Vote in California*, from the Anne Martin Papers, F863.S8, p. 56, courtesy of The Bancroft Library, University of California, Berkeley.

Aaron Augustus Sargent, a pioneering California politician, congressional representative, and US senator. Photograph by William Shew, c. 1860. From the California Faces Collection, courtesy of The Bancroft Library, University of California, Berkeley; Sargent, Aaron A–POR 1.

ratified, providing unrestricted voting rights for women. The amendment owes much to the efforts of two close friends of Susan B. Anthony: Aaron and Ellen Sargent of Nevada City.

Aaron Augustus Sargent was born in Newburyport, Massachusetts, in 1827. As a boy he was apprenticed to a cabinetmaker, but he yearned to be a printer. While still in his teens, he met his future wife, Ellen Clark, when they taught Sunday school together in Newburyport. Abandoning cabinetry, Sargent learned the printing trade, and he worked as a printer in Philadelphia before moving, in 1847, to Washington, DC, where he served as secretary to a member of Congress. Just barely in his twenties, he continued to court Ellen, pledging to marry her when his circumstances and finances permitted. It would take the California Gold Rush to make his vow a reality.

After gold was discovered in California, Sargent borrowed $125 from his uncle and sailed to California from Baltimore in 1849. Following a long boat voyage to San Francisco and months as a vagabond miner in Gold Country, Sargent arrived in the rough Sierra camp then simply called Nevada. (The town would be renamed Nevada City in the 1860s.) He failed as a miner so, drawing upon his printing experience, he turned his efforts to publishing, founding the *Nevada Journal* newspaper. As did most newspapers of the era, the *Nevada Journal* had pronounced political leanings, in this case strongly advocating Whig Party policies.

Sargent returned to Massachusetts to marry Ellen Clark on March 15, 1852, and together the couple returned to Nevada City in October of that year. Upon arrival, Ellen was pleased to discover that her husband had a house. It was a one-story, four-room dwelling with ceilings covered by muslin. Ellen Clark Sargent loved the comfortable home, except for one very noticeable annoyance:

> I call to mind the little, or rather big animals, which used
> to call down themselves the maledictions of the would
> be neat and tidy housewife. I refer to the large sized
> rats which made their nests and performed their activi-
> ties on the dark side of the muslin above our heads.

Meanwhile, work was tense for Aaron Sargent, as competing news-papers with opposing political viewpoints published vitriolic editorials critical of the *Nevada Journal*'s Whig Party sentiments. One rival paper, the *Young America*, edited by R. A. Davridge, had a strong Democratic Party bias and found the *Nevada Journal* particularly offensive. Before cooler heads prevailed, Davridge threatened to shoot Aaron.

While editing the *Nevada Journal*, Aaron also studied law. In 1854 he was admitted to the bar, and in 1856 he began a political career as the elected district attorney of Nevada County. With the founding of the Republican Party in 1854, many former Whigs joined the new orga-nization, and Aaron became an important leader of the Republicans. In 1860, he was vice president of the Republican National Conven-tion that selected Abraham Lincoln as its presidential candidate. In that same year, Aaron was elected to the House of Representatives, where he would serve three terms—from 1861 to 1863 and from 1869 to 1873.

As chairman of the House Railroad Committee in 1862, Aaron au-thored the Pacific Railroad Act, which sanctioned the construction of the Transcontinental Railroad. On April 10, 1862, he presented a full-throated defense of the act in a speech before Congress: "I believe…this bill is more perfect in its provisions than any ever before submitted to the attention of Congress….By a single act you can send a thrill of joy through the Pacific States…and you will deserve for this Congress the name of the wisest and most far-seeing of any that has convened since the formation of the Government."

While Aaron Sargent was pursuing his political career, Ellen Clark Sargent was following her interest in women's rights. During her life-time, women had few and severely restricted rights. While there were local variations, women generally could not vote, hold office, or attend professional schools. They earned lower wages than men for equal labor and endured unsafe working conditions in factories. Except in a few localities such as New York, married women were not allowed to make contracts, control any wages they might earn, devise wills, or own property.

Ellen was outraged and vowed to convey to women "the great privi-leges and responsibilities of full American citizenship," as she expressed in a letter to her friend and prominent women's rights advocate Sarah Willis of Palo Alto. She continued:

> Does not that apply to women as well as men? Why cannot women see their low estate in the scale of humanity! And to think they could change it if they would. How their condition argues against their mentality and self-respect. Why do they not blush and arise in their might and inaugurate a true republic in keeping with this enlightened age?

In 1869, Ellen founded the first women's suffrage group in Nevada City. She attended many meetings, circulated a suffrage petition that was presented to the California State Legislature in 1870, and came to be a widely respected leader in the movement. Ellen was a friend and colleague to many of the important national suffrage leaders, most notably Susan B. Anthony, who was a frequent visitor to the Sargent home in Washington, DC. During their residency in the nation's capital, Ellen was the most conspicuous suffragist among congressional wives, ultimately serving for six years as treasurer of the National American Woman Suffrage Association, the most influential women's rights organization of its day. She was also the Honorary President of the California Equal Suffrage Association.

In 1872, Aaron was elected to the United States Senate, where he would serve one term and earn the nickname "the Senator for the Southern Pacific Railroad" for his continued advocacy of the project. But the railroad was not his only focus, and in 1878, influenced by Ellen, her friend Susan B. Anthony, and others in the suffrage movement, Senator Sargent introduced the twenty-eight words that later became the Nineteenth Amendment to the Constitution:

> The right of citizens of the United States to vote shall not be denied or abridged by the United States or by any State on account of sex.

The bill calling for the constitutional amendment would be introduced and then summarily dismissed each year for the next forty years.

Following Aaron's Senate service, the Sargents returned to California in 1880, and Aaron died in 1887, at the age of fifty-nine. He was originally buried in San Francisco's Laurel Hill Cemetery, but when commercial construction overtook the property, his ashes were disinterred and scattered over his mining claims, and his vault was moved to Nevada City's Pioneer Cemetery, just a few hundred yards from where he had built Ellen's muslin-covered Gold Rush home.

Ellen Clark Sargent continued her political activism, and in 1896 she was a leader in promoting an ultimately unsuccessful ballot initiative granting voting rights to California women. In 1900, the seventy-four-year-old Ellen went to court to protest the payment of her property taxes; since she was not allowed to vote, she argued she was a victim of "taxation without representation." She lost her case but made a powerful public statement. Inspired by her example, other suffragists brought similar court actions in following years.

Ellen enthusiastically supported the women's suffrage cause until her death in San Francisco on July 13, 1911. On July 26, 1911, more than one thousand people gathered at her memorial service in Union Square. Among those who expressed their condolences were notables such as California governor Hiram Johnson and Stanford University president David Starr Jordan. San Francisco mayor Patrick McCarthy ordered all city flags flown at half-staff in her honor—the first time a woman was so honored. At the service, numerous speakers recalled Ellen Clark Sargent's long commitment to the cause of equal rights, and they urged Californians to support women's voting rights in the upcoming October election. Elizabeth Lowe Watson, president of the California Equal Suffrage Association from 1909 to 1911, stated:

> [Ellen Clark Sargent] was a firm believer in the principles
> of pure democracy, in a government of, by and for the
> people—men and women alike. She was one of the first
> and foremost to demand and work for enfranchisement
> of her sex, but her eloquence lay more in deeds than in
> words....It was her strong conviction that the ballot, in the
> hands of women, would help redeem the world, and, to
> this end,...she gave freely of her substance and herself.

On October 10, 1911, just a few months after Ellen's death, Californians voted in favor of women's suffrage. On August 26, 1920, the

Nineteenth Amendment to the United States Constitution was ratified, granting women the right to vote in all elections. It used exactly the same wording that Senator Aaron Augustus Sargent had introduced forty years earlier.

Aaron A. Sargent and the Chinese Exclusion Act

Considering his advocacy of the women's suffrage amendment, it is surprising that California senator Aaron Sargent was an ardent proponent of one of the most prohibitive laws in all of American history: the Chinese Exclusion Act of 1882, which restricted Chinese laborers from entering the United States for a period of ten years and barred Chinese immigrants from gaining citizenship, voting privileges, and other customary civil rights.

From his first days in the US Senate, Sargent spoke against the continued presence of the Chinese in California, which had by far the largest state population of Chinese immigrants. In 1876, he gave an anti-Chinese speech on the floor of the Senate that was published and widely distributed. This excerpt captures the thrust of his speech:

> [The Chinese are] swarming millions of men, alien not
> alone to our blood and our language, but to our faith....
> Chinamen, as a race, are addicted to all the nameless vices
> characteristic of the Asiatics....The Chinaman can live on a
> dead rat and a few handfuls of rice [and] work for ten cents
> a day....There can be no remedy except general exclusion.

In 1878, Sargent railed against Chinese immigration, stating that it "presents as great a present evil as any ever ascribed to slavery in the southern States."

A damaged wet-plate portrait of Aaron A. Sargent, former United States senator from California. Photograph by Matthew Brady, c. 1880. From the Brady-Handy Photograph Collection, 1865–1880, courtesy of the Library of Congress, Prints and Photographs Division, Washington, DC, LC-DIG-cwpbh-04511.

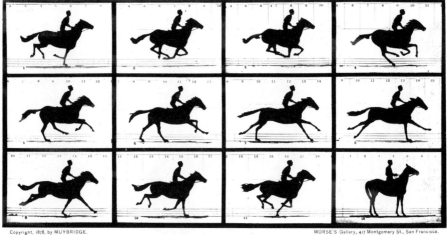

MORSE'S Gallery, 417 Montgomery St., San Francisco.

THE HORSE IN MOTION

Illustrated by
MUYBRIDGE.

AUTOMATIC ELECTRO-PHOTOGRAPH

"SALLIE GARDNER," owned by LELAND STANFORD; running at a 1.40 gait over the Palo Alto track, 19th June, 1878.

The negatives of these photographs were made at intervals of twenty-seven inches of distance, and about the twenty-fifth part of a second of time; they illustrate consecutive positions assumed in each twenty-seven inches of progress during a single stride of the mare. The vertical lines were twenty-seven inches apart; the horizontal lines represent elevations of four inches each. The exposure of each negative was less than the two-thousandth part of a second.

PHOTOGRAPHIC MEMORY

Eadweard Muybridge

Deep in the recesses of the California State Library in Sacramento is an inner sanctum, a vault that holds the most precious jewels of the library. On a shelf in this diminutive room is a very rare book entitled *Yosemite: Its Wonders and Its Beauties.* Published in 1868, it is generally believed that fewer than six copies of the volume survive. Most consider it the first guidebook to Yosemite. And while the story of the book is interesting, that of the photographer is no less unique.

Yosemite: Its Wonders and Its Beauties was written by newspaper correspondent and editor John Shertzer Hittell and included helpful maps and a list of attractions. Hittell hoped to convince a national audience

"The Horse in Motion," the most famous motion-study photographic series produced by Eadweard Muybridge, 1878. Illustration by Muybridge of Sallie Gardner, owned by Leland Stanford, running at a 1:40 gait over the Palo Alto track, June 19, 1878. Courtesy of the Library of Congress, Prints and Photographs Division, Washington, DC, LC-DIG-ppmsca-23778.

of the extraordinary beauty of this natural wonder, so, rather than rely-
ing on a painter's interpretation, Hittell hired an up-and-coming but
rather eccentric photographer named Eadweard Muybridge to take images of Yosemite Valley for inclusion in the guidebook. Photos were
necessary, Hittell insisted, "because no engravings could do justice to
the scenes, or convey perfect confidence in the accuracy of the drawing of such immense elevations as those of Tutucanala [El Capitan] and
Tissayac [Half Dome]."

Muybridge leapt at the chance. He hiked hundreds of miles with all
the required equipment—the bulky cameras of the day, and gallons of
chemicals—an endeavor that necessitated wagons, assistants, a sturdy
back, and a faithful mule. The process of taking the photos was difficult, but it was after he had finished preparing the photographic plates
that the real hard work began. Muybridge and his assistants developed
and printed hundreds and hundreds of original photographs, and each
one had to be laboriously pasted—or "tipped"—into the guidebook by
hand. *Yosemite: Its Wonders and Its Beauties* is remembered today for its
historical value and rarity, but it is only one part of Muybridge's legacy.

Publishing his photographs under the pseudonym "Helios"—the
Greek god of the Sun—Eadweard Muybridge helped spread the word
of the amazing wonderland that is Yosemite, but he was even better
known for his photos of animal and human locomotion. Utilizing multiple cameras and tripwire shutters, Muybridge took dozens of serial
photos of subjects in motion and then put them together in film strips.
His most famous series was of a galloping horse, and the photos were
used to settle a friendly wager (and to gain respect in horse racing and
breeding circles) by the powerful railroad baron and politician Leland
Stanford as to whether a horse lifted all four of its hooves at the same
time while running. Stanford asserted that they do and Muybridge
proved him correct.

Muybridge's eye was interested in motion studies of all kinds. He
snapped photos of a couple dancing, a buffalo galloping, a worker
wielding a pick, a baboon climbing a pole, a cat leaping, a nude man
running, a horse and buggy in full trot, and many more. Cut into strips
and placed in a circular viewing device called a zoetrope, the photos

could be spun rapidly to produce the illusion of movement, much like a flip book. A more sophisticated viewer was the praxinoscope, which utilized mirrors to achieve the same effect. When the praxinoscope was coupled with a gadget of Muybridge's design—the zoopraxiscope—the images could be seen by a crowd instead of just a single person. It could be considered the first movie projector. Using these machines, audiences were able to see photographs come to life right before their eyes. They stood in awe as they watched two dogs tugging at a towel, the passing of two well-dressed women on the street, a spirited game of leapfrog, and dozens of other scenes, including the first moving images of a man being kicked by a mule. As a result of these innovative techniques and applications, Muybridge is considered one of the fathers of the motion picture and a pioneer of animation.

Professional accomplishments aside, Muybridge's personal life would have been an excellent subject for a movie, if movies had existed during his time. Born Edward James Muggeridge on April 9, 1830, in Kingston upon Thames, England, he left for America as a young man and changed his name several times as an adult, eventually settling on Eadweard Muybridge because he believed it was the proper Anglo-Saxon spelling. He made a name for himself as an early photographer of Yosemite Valley, and by the 1870s, he was not only a widely celebrated photographer but also the most scandalous.

In 1874, Muybridge discovered that his wife had a lover, Major Harry Larkyns. On October 17, Muybridge sought out Larkyns and, confronting him, said, "Good evening, Major, my name is Muybridge and here's the answer to the letter you sent my wife." Muybridge then pulled out a shotgun and killed Larkyns. At his murder trial, the defense offered a plea of insanity due to a head injury Muybridge had sustained following a stagecoach accident. Friends testified that the accident had dramatically altered Muybridge's personality and made him volatile and unpredictable. The jury dismissed the insanity plea, but the defendant was ultimately acquitted for "justifiable homicide." Leland Stanford paid for Muybridge's criminal defense. A few months after his acquittal, Muybridge's then ex-wife died, and Muybridge, convinced that his son, Florado Helios Muybridge, had been fathered by Larkyns, disowned the young boy and placed him in an orphanage. It is said that when the boy grew up, he bore a striking resemblance to...Muybridge.

In early 1875, Muybridge left the United States and photographed in Central America under yet another assumed name—Eduardo Santiago Muybridge. He returned to the United States from his self-imposed exile in 1877 and continued his motion studies, published several popular books, and lectured throughout the world. In addition to their influence on motion pictures and animation, Muybridge's groundbreaking serial motion studies are also considered to have been vital to the development of special effects photography, biomechanics, and athletic physiology.

Muybridge returned permanently to England in 1894, and he died ten years later, at age seventy-four, in his hometown of Kingston upon Thames. On his grave marker, his last name is spelled differently once again—this time, the final time, as Maybridge.

SIERRA SPOTLIGHT

Carleton Watkins

Carleton Watkins, a native of upstate New York, came to California in 1851. Upon his arrival, Watkins became fascinated by the new artistic medium of photography and began taking his own images in 1858. He experimented with several photographic techniques but soon came to favor what he called his "Mammoth Camera," which used large glass-plate negatives to produce prints much larger than could be created on standard equipment of the era. In 1861 Watkins traveled to Yosemite equipped with his Mammoth as well as a stereographic camera. His colossal prints and stereographic views of Yosemite Valley were very influential in convincing Congress to grant national park status to Yosemite.

Carleton Watkins established a lavish photography studio in San Francisco, but bad business practices led to hard times. Watkins never lacked for work, but he also never prospered, and for a short time, his family had to live in an abandoned railroad car. Then his eyesight began to fade.

In 1906, the final blow occurred. In the devastating San Francisco earthquake and fire of that year, Watkins watched as his studio and the vast majority of his prints, plates, and negatives were destroyed in a massive fire. A poignant photograph shows the distraught photographer fleeing the flames. He never recovered from the loss, and in 1910 he was admitted to the Napa State Hospital for the Insane, where he died six years later at the age of eighty-six.

Celebrated photographer Carleton Watkins, with cane, fleeing from the flames during the aftermath of the Great San Francisco Earthquake, April 18, 1906. From the San Francisco Earthquake and Fire Collection, courtesy of The Bancroft Library, University of California, Berkeley; Watkins, Carleton E.–POR 1.

THE UNKNOWN ARCHITECT

John Conness

For decades, the precipitous walls of Yosemite Valley have been an enticement for daring climbers. But they would not be available for either the adventurous mountaineer or the more timid onlooker if it were not for the efforts of one man: John Conness, quite likely the most influential yet anonymous figure in Sierra Nevada history. You may not know his name, but you know his handiwork—Yosemite Valley. John Conness was a critical participant in the establishment of a government-controlled Yosemite as well as in the forging of the ideal that led to its ultimate status as a national park.

Conness was born in Ireland in 1821 and immigrated to the United States in 1836. Barely surviving in New York City, he joined the thousands of hopeful goldseekers headed to California in 1849. As did many

John Conness, United States senator from California and author of the Yosemite Valley Grant Act of 1864. Photograph by Matthew Brady, c. 1865. From the Brady-Handy Photograph Collection, 1855–1865, courtesy of the Library of Congress, Prints and Photographs Division, Washington, DC, LC-DIG-cwpbh-01372.

other forty-niners, Conness found gold mining a difficult pursuit, and he soon settled for selling supplies to miners, becoming a merchant in the little Sierra community of Georgetown.

During the early years of California's statehood, the Georgetown merchant gravitated toward politics. Conness served in the California State Legislature and ran unsuccessfully for both lieutenant governor and governor in 1859 and 1861, respectively. In 1863, the gregarious Conness was selected by the California State Legislature to serve as the state's US senator.

On March 28, 1864, Conness introduced Senate Bill 203—the Yosemite Valley Grant Act—which would grant to the State of California the Yosemite Valley and the Mariposa Grove of Big Trees. In his passionate endorsement of the bill, Conness famously stated that the grant areas would be "for all public purposes worthless, but…constitute, perhaps, some of the greatest wonders of the world.…[T]he property shall be inalienable forever, and preserved and improved as a place of public resort."

No money was appropriated in support of the bill, and no supporting legislation provided for federal administration of the areas. It did not establish the National Park—that would come later, in 1890—but it did inaugurate the concept that protecting places of natural beauty should be a national priority, an idea that ultimately led to the founding of the first national park at Yellowstone in 1872. The concept of protected national parks would spread to the rest of the world and inspire the establishment of many similar refuges. It is arguably the best American export.

The Yosemite Valley Grant Act passed both houses of Congress after only a few hours of debate, and on June 30, 1864, during the depths of the bloody Civil War, it was signed into law by President Abraham Lincoln. Conness and Lincoln held each other in high regard, and Conness was a pallbearer at the president's funeral the following year. Conness himself only served one term in the Senate and then retired to Boston, living to the age of eighty-seven.

John Conness is commemorated by several landmarks in the Sierra Nevada, including the Conness Glacier and the nearly 13,000-foot Mount Conness, near the Yosemite boundary.

SIERRA SPOTLIGHT

Galen Clark

Senator John Conness introduced the legislation that brought Yosemite Valley under government protection, but the idea actually belonged to Galen Clark. Born in 1814, Clark, a native of Canada, migrated to Missouri as a youth, and after the death of his young wife, he headed to California in 1848. In 1853, he suffered a lung hemorrhage and was told his days were numbered. His doctor prescribed rest and clean mountain air,

so Clark set off for the Sierra Nevada, to a little community he knew in Mariposa County named Wawona. One of the earliest non-natives to visit the nearby Mariposa Grove of giant sequoias, Clark was the first European American to count and measure the massive trees there. He wrote letter after letter to friends and members of Congress, seeking protection for the grove and the valley. He found his greatest supporter in Senator John Conness, who introduced the Yosemite Valley Grant Act in 1864. He was named the first official "Guardian of the Grove," a position he held for more than thirty years. To his credit, Clark did not attempt to profit from his role in the establishment of Yosemite and he struggled financially as a tour guide and hotelier. He ultimately sold Clark's Station, which later became the location of today's Wawona Hotel. Clark died in 1910 at the age of ninety-five, a mere fifty-seven years after a doctor said he had a few months to live. He is buried in Yosemite Valley, at a site he chose, surrounded by sequoia trees he had planted.

Galen Clark, Guardian of the Mariposa Grove. From a stereograph by Carleton Watkins, c. 1870. From the series "Photographic Views of California, Oregon, and the Pacific Coast, c. 1865," No. 1174, courtesy of the Library of Congress, Prints and Photographs Division, Washington, DC, LC-DIG-stereo-1s00445.

GLORIOUS STARRY FIRMAMENT FOR A ROOF

Pioneering Yosemite Rock Climbers

Once Yosemite Valley came under government control in 1864, visitors flocked to the area to recreate and commune. The gleaming granite cliffs, knobs, and spires were a magnet for the audacious and, perhaps, foolhardy. The question became Could these majestic rocks be climbed, or was it silly to even consider the attempt? Experts of all stripes contemplated the possibilities, and most decided that ascending these heights was impossible. In 1870, Josiah Whitney, a world-renowned scientist, Harvard professor, and California's state geologist, stated that Half Dome "never has been and never will be trodden by

George Anderson perched on the rim of Half Dome in Yosemite Valley. In 1875, Anderson became the first person to climb Half Dome. From a stereograph published by Martin M. Hazeltine; photograph attributed to Selah Clarence Walker, 1877. Courtesy of the New York Public Library.

human foot," and that the summit of the imposing formation was "perfectly inaccessible."

But one man who lived in a tiny log cabin in Yosemite Valley thought otherwise. He was George Anderson, a Scotsman by birth and a ship's carpenter by trade and experience. He believed the glacially polished surface of Half Dome could be conquered and the seemingly inaccessible summit reached.

Anderson was not the first to attempt the climb, however. John Conway, employed for many years in Yosemite to construct trails and roads, had dispatched some workers to make the ascent; one account by John Muir refers to them as a "flock of small boys who climb smooth rocks like lizards." They made it partway up, but when they failed to make the final steep, slick journey to the top, they abandoned the effort.

In October 1875, Anderson started up that final grade of Half Dome wearing his boots, but when he found they lacked sufficient grip, he resorted to climbing barefoot. That method ultimately proved ineffective as well, and in the 1888 book *In the Heart of the Sierras*, Yosemite Valley witness James Hutchings recalled Anderson's next move:

> [Anderson] tied sacking upon his feet and legs, but as
> these did not secure the desired object, he covered it
> with pitch, obtained from pine trees near; and although
> this enabled him to adhere firmly to the smooth granite,
> and effectually prevented him from slipping, a new diffi-
> culty presented itself in the great effort required to unstick
> himself and which came near proving fatal several times.

Then sufficiently sticky, the pine-pitch-plastered Anderson began drilling holes in the granite and inserting iron eyebolts through which he looped a climbing rope. He would stand on the eyebolt he had just placed, drill the hole for the next one, insert another bolt, loop the rope, and so on—up about one thousand feet in total. It took Anderson several days, but finally, as Hutchings reported, "with dint of pluck, unswerving perseverance, and personal daring," he at last reached his goal at 3 p.m. on October 12, 1875.

Others would soon follow. A group of English tourists scrambled up Half Dome using Anderson's rope within days of that first ascent. A day or two after that, the adventurous Sarah Dutcher, who had come to California via Tasmania and Honolulu and was working in the valley selling photographs, was the first woman to climb the rock, assisted by Anderson. Julius Birge, a friend of Anderson's, remarked that she was "certainly the first and possibly the last woman who made the ascent."

Anderson hoped to capitalize on his success by building a staircase to the top of Half Dome and escorting tourists to the summit...for a fee, of course. He worked on the staircase, but a series of massive snowstorms swept away any progress he made. John Muir, who made his first ascent of Half Dome only a few weeks after Anderson's, roundly denounced any effort to commercialize the iconic Yosemite feature. In a newspaper article from November 1875, in which he referred to Half Dome by two commonly used names of the time period—South Dome and Tissiack—Muir stated:

> I have always discouraged as much as possible every project for laddering the South Dome, believing it would be a fine thing to keep this garden untrodden....When a mountain is climbed it is said to be conquered—as well say a man is conquered when a fly lights on his head. Blue jays have trodden the Dome many a day; so have beetles and chipmunks, and Tissiack will hardly be more conquered, now that man is added to her list of visitors.

Anderson died in 1884 from pneumonia. He is buried in the Yosemite Pioneer Cemetery, in the shadow of Half Dome.

Today, thousands of Yosemite visitors scale Half Dome each year using a cable pathway to the summit. On warm summer days, there's practically a traffic jam on the "perfectly inaccessible" monolith.

SIERRA SPOTLIGHT

A. Phimister Proctor

Modern rock climbers use a sophisticated array of equipment carefully engineered for safety and efficiency, ranging from high-tech ropes to heat-hardened carabiners to specialized climbing shoes. But in the earliest days of mountaineering, the technique was pretty much hang on and hope. One heart-pounding example of this method was the scaling of Half Dome in 1884 by twenty-four-year-old Alexander Phimister Proctor.

Proctor had been challenged by early conservationist Galen Clark to reestablish the rope line to the Half Dome summit strung by George Anderson in 1875. In the nine years since Anderson's ascent, the rope had rotted away and the iron eyebolts had rusted, and Proctor agreed he was the man for the job. Proctor abandoned his boots and climbed barefoot from one potentially disintegrating eyebolt to the next. As Proctor described: "I was standing on a two-inch bolt, with my big toe the only support between me and the valley below. There was never a handhold." To reach the next eyebolt, Proctor would fling a rope and attempt to lasso it. Sometimes it would take him thirty minutes to successfully snag the bolt. The rope used was also his horse rope, which was thin and frayed, but sometimes it was actually too strong for the job and occasionally a good tug would dislodge an eyebolt, which would tumble crazily to the valley floor below.

After two harrowing days, Proctor and his climbing companion reached the top of Half Dome. They built a fire to signal their success to waiting observers in the valley below. As Proctor recalled years later: "There are times in a young man's life that a great experience changes it. Those two days on Half Dome were for me the divide between careless youth and serious manhood." Proctor abandoned rock climbing forever after his Half Dome ordeal and began a career as a prominent sculptor.

A self-portrait of A. Phimister Proctor ascending Half Dome in 1884. Drawing first published in 1945. Courtesy of The Bancroft Library, University of California, Berkeley, 19xx.260—B.

THE FIRST LIGHT OF EVENING

The Folsom Powerhouse

During California State Fair Week in 1879, Sacramento residents were treated to a flash of the future. The *Sacramento Union* and the Weinstock, Lubin, and Company department store sponsored a public exhibit of electric lighting, and nearly five thousand visitors came to see the display of sizzling and dangerous arc lights and then clamored for electric power in the state capital. The prospect was difficult to envision in the 1880s; electricity was inefficient and expensive to generate, since it utilized batteries or coal-powered steam engines, which transmitted only limited power over a short range. At the time, it was used only for devices that required very little power, such as telegraphs, telephones, and burglar alarms.

The California State Capitol fully illuminated for Sacramento's Grand Electric Carnival, celebrated on Admission Day, September 9, 1895. Courtesy of the Sacramento Public Library, Sacramento Room, Image 2389.

But electric power was clearly the wave of the future. After the incandescent lightbulb was introduced to Sacramento in 1890, the call for electricity increased dramatically. Soon, the State Capitol had installed outlets for fourteen hundred electric lights, and despite the exorbitant cost of coal to run steam dynamos, the Southern Pacific Railroad also converted their shops to electricity. Still, a mechanism to produce inexpensive and abundant energy remained elusive. One technique that seemed favorable was hydroelectricity, by which electric power is created by water turbines.

In the 1860s, the Natoma Water and Mining Company, a firm near Folsom, started building an extensive network of dams, ditches, and reservoirs to supply water to mines on the American River. The owner, Horatio Gates Livermore, wished to dam the river and create sawmill holding ponds. The project was enormously costly and required significant quarrying and construction, but it promised to be so valuable that the State of California agreed to supply convicts from nearby Folsom Prison as a labor force. The work proceeded slowly, and by the 1880s, Livermore had died and the company was controlled by his two sons, Horatio P. and Charles Livermore. The sons revised the project and embraced the possibility of the site being used to generate hydroelectric power. At the time, a handful of hydroelectric plants had been constructed in Germany and New York, and a few hydraulic mines in the Sierra Nevada had even experimented with the process in the 1880s, but these were rare, small-scale experiments. The Livermore brothers had bigger plans. They would dig a 9,500-foot canal that would provide water power to four of the largest electrical generators, or dynamos, ever constructed. In 1895, the *Journal of Electricity* exclaimed, "These are without doubt the largest three-phase dynamos yet constructed." Each dynamo was more than eight feet tall, weighed in excess of fifty-seven thousand pounds, featured 1260-horsepower dual turbines, and could produce 750 kilowatts. They were driven by eight-foot-diameter penstocks using water from the American River. Construction on the hydroelectric facility began in 1894.

By 1895, the brick Folsom Powerhouse was completed and ready to transmit electricity to Sacramento, twenty-two miles away, a distance far greater than electricity had ever been distributed. The Livermore brothers and their new partner, Albert Gallatin, president of the Huntington-Hopkins Hardware Company of Sacramento, anticipated great success and vast profits.

The partners decided to announce the arrival of electric power in Sacramento with a theatrical flourish. At 4 a.m. on July 13, 1895, slumbering residents were awakened with a one-hundred-gun salute followed by the declaration that electricity had been conveyed—over uninsulated copper wire—from Folsom. It was the first time that high-voltage alternating current had been successfully conducted over a long distance and was undoubtedly a groundbreaking scientific and engineering accomplishment.

On September 9, 1895, California observed Admission Day, a holiday marking the state's entrance into the Union in 1850, and it was on that occasion in Sacramento that officials also celebrated the arrival of cheap electric power by staging an elaborate "Grand Electrical Carnival," which featured lights strung along downtown thoroughfares and a State Capitol decorated with thousands of incandescent bulbs. The next day, the *Sacramento Bee* reported that over sixty thousand people had witnessed the spectacular display:

> Sacramento's pulse beat high and fast last night. She had cast aside the old and faded robes of her humble childhood days and stood at the new altar of celestial fire to be made the bride of Progress of the new century that is about to dawn.... Twenty-five thousand incandescent lamps, in the cherry red, apple green and orange tints of the carnival made the streets and upper air ablaze with light....They outlined the cornices, the roof, and every column, balcony and rib of the great dome of the Capitol building up to the bird cage at the top.

Using the same basic equipment as it began with in 1895, the Folsom Powerhouse continued in operation until 1952, when it was replaced by the hydroelectric plant at the recently completed Folsom Dam. In 1958, the powerhouse complex was acquired by the California Department of Parks and Recreation, and the Livermore brothers' original structure has since been designated a National Historic

Civil Engineering Landmark (1975) and a National Historic Mechanical Engineering Landmark (1976), and it was chosen as California Historical Landmark #633. In 1981, the Powerhouse was also listed on the National Register of Historic Places.

SIERRA SPOTLIGHT

French Corral and the Telephone

The Gold Rush town of French Corral is celebrated as the site of the world's first long-distance telephone line. Alexander Graham Bell received the patent for the telephone in March 1876, and the French Corral connection was established in 1878. Constructed by the Edison Company at a cost of $6,000, the sixty-mile link united the offices of three mining companies in the region, stretching from French Corral eastward to French Lake (now called Bowman Lake). Between them, the three companies owned and developed more than 320 miles and $5 million worth of ditches and flumes, which supplied the copious amounts of water necessary for their hydraulic mining ventures. The telephone system allowed the firms to coordinate and regulate flow from Sierra Nevada reservoirs.

1407. FRENCH CORRAL MINING CAMP—Nevada Co.

French Corral, the tiny Nevada County mining camp that was the location of the world's first long-distance telephone line in 1876. Photograph by Lawrence and Houseworth, c. 1870. From the Lawrence and Houseworth Collection, courtesy of the Society of California Pioneers, San Francisco, Image # 1136 (SCP).

MAGNIFICENT SCOUNDREL

Lucky Baldwin

One of the most colorful figures in the history of the American West was a reckless gambler, an immoral schemer, a four-time husband (who was shot *twice* by jilted lovers), and also a clever businessman, an astute investor, a real estate genius, a savior of part of Lake Tahoe, and one of the richest men of the nineteenth century.

Lucky Baldwin, as he was known, was born Elias Jackson Baldwin in Ohio in 1828 and spent his childhood in Indiana and Wisconsin. Growing up, Baldwin developed a reputation as a peripatetic opportunist and a shrewd, and perhaps shady, businessman. He left Wisconsin for the Gold Rush, arriving in 1853 in San Francisco, where he opened a hotel and livery stable and almost immediately made a profit, which he then sank into investments, particularly in mining. In payment for a debt, he received two thousand shares in a mine near Virginia City

Colorful character Elias Jackson "Lucky" Baldwin enjoys a spirited card game, c. 1895. From the California History Room Picture Collection: Elias Baldwin, no. 2008-0882, courtesy of the California State Library, Sacramento.

called the Ophir Mine, and although at the time the stock was worth pennies and was not expected to amount to anything, it suddenly became a moneymaker when the adjacent Comstock Lode was discovered in 1859. Baldwin's stock value and personal wealth increased overnight. In short order, through a combination of judicious investments, excellent timing, and more than a little good fortune, E. J. Baldwin became well-to-do.

Baldwin parlayed his mining investments into huge real estate holdings. He accumulated six thousand acres in Bear Valley, eight thousand acres at Lake Tahoe, business holdings in San Francisco and Los Angeles, and sixty-three thousand acres in Southern California, including the land where the present-day cities of Arcadia and Monrovia are located. Many snickered that Baldwin had purchased worthless badlands in the southern part of the state that were useful only for limited animal grazing, but once again, Lucky was lucky. On his Merced pastureland, oil was discovered and the property was developed into the Montebello Oil Fields, one of the richest strikes in the west. On the so-called Baldwin Hills, Lucky grazed sheep for decades until another oil strike yielded millions. On his Santa Anita Ranch, he constructed the original Santa Anita Racetrack and became a California pioneer in thoroughbred horse breeding and racing. The renovated track is still on Baldwin estate land.

A bit of a scoundrel, Baldwin's matrimonial adventures were public scandals. He was married four times and sued by four other paramours for "breach of promise to marry." One of his accusers received $75,000 in damages, while two exacted their revenge more directly: Baldwin was shot by one of his complainants in 1883, and the brother of another rejected suitor wounded Baldwin with a pistol blast a few years later.

In 1933, C. B. Glasscock, Lucky Baldwin's biographer, described him as "perhaps the outstanding individualist of his generation in America—indifferent to convention, scornful of public opinion, defiant of restriction, acquisitive, energetic, immoral, successful according to his own lights."

Today, Baldwin's name and legacy is found in many places in California, particularly in the Los Angeles region. The Baldwin Hills District of Los Angeles, the City of Baldwin Park, Baldwin Avenue in the San

Gabriel Valley, and the Baldwin Stakes horserace at Santa Anita are all named after this one-of-a-kind character.

During the 1870s, the rollicking Baldwin had invested heavily in the Comstock Lode, and during his visits to Virginia City to attend to his mining interests he became charmed by the beauty and the commercial prospects of Lake Tahoe, which he had first seen on a pack-train in 1853.

Baldwin stopped at a small resort on the lake's south shore called Yank's. The proprietor was Ephraim "Yank" Clement, a homesteading immigrant from Maine, who had expanded his original homestead to include one thousand acres near the lake. Founded in 1875, Yank's Resort, as it was called, featured a thick forest that stretched back from the shoreline. By the 1870s, such lush vegetation was beginning to vanish from the area. To feed the never-ending hunger for timber of the railroad and Comstock Lode ventures, Lake Tahoe had been stripped of its virgin forests and was quickly becoming a hideous, stumpy waste-land. Even Baldwin, a capitalist to his marrow, was outraged by the waste. Upon seeing the devastation, he supposedly exclaimed to Yank, "By gad! It's a shame and a crime! Some one will be cutting this timber next," waving his hand at Yank's untouched forestland.

Baldwin decided to act. In 1881, he purchased Yank's thousand-acre property and began a wily process that would ultimately secure an additional seven thousand neighboring acres. He renamed the resort Tallac, in honor of the perpetually snow-adorned peak that overlooked the property. Although he had managed to save the trees, true to form, Baldwin's motives were not purely altruistic; he expanded the resort to ten times its previous capacity, built the lavish Tallac House hotel and casino, and ushered in twenty-seven years of profitable luxury by the lake.

Baldwin's Tallac House shamelessly proclaimed itself the "Summer Resort of the World," with "cuisine equal to any, excelled by none." The ballroom featured a spring-mounted dance floor that forced the guests to dance "whether they knew or not." The resort's brochure proudly exclaimed that "to obtain the air the angels breathe, you must go to Tahoe"—a sentiment echoing Mark Twain's famous description of the lake's atmosphere in *Roughing It*: "The air up there in the clouds is very pure and fine, bracing and delicious. And why shouldn't it be?—it is the same the angels breathe."

Tallac House also featured gambling, as did every other resort circling Lake Tahoe. Gambling was illegal, but regulation was lax, and raids by local law enforcement were anticipated well in advance, giving the proprietors plenty of time to hide the large primitive slot machines and poker tables.

In 1909, Lucky Baldwin died. Few relatives attended his funeral, and as the *San Francisco Call* account of the service tellingly reported, "There was little grief....The wall of the violins was not jarred by a sob." Soon afterward, his heirs began to dismantle the Lake Tahoe resort and transform it into a private estate. In 1915, Dextra Baldwin Winter, Baldwin's granddaughter, obtained the title to the hotel grounds and reconstructed it as her permanent private summer residence. Winter's U-shaped building, completed in 1922, sported the finest materials, workmanship, and design, and featured an inviting courtyard wishing well, incense cedar framing, and hand-forged wrought iron fixtures.

Today the Baldwin Estate is part of the glimmering Tallac Historic Site, which comprises three adjoining "Old Tahoe" properties: the Tevis-Pope, Heller, and Baldwin Estates. The splendid setting encompasses seventy-four acres and includes more than four hundred yards of lakeside frontage. The Tallac Historic Site was formally established in the early 1970s and is listed on the National Register of Historic Places. It is open to the public.

SIERRA SPOTLIGHT

The State Line Country Club

In Lucky Baldwin's day, casino gambling was illegal in both California and Nevada and had to be conducted with some degree of stealth, but that all changed in 1931, when Nevada legalized gambling. All around Lake Tahoe's eastern shore, gambling establishments sprung up at or near the state boundary. The first casino of consequence was the State Line Country Club, in Stateline, Nevada. At the borderline, the com-

The State Line Country Club was the first major casino at Lake Tahoe following Nevada's legalization of gambling in 1931. This is the current location of Harrah's Lake Tahoe. Photograph by Frasher Fotos. From the Images of Lake Tahoe Collection, courtesy of the Special Collections Department, University of Nevada, Reno, UNRS-P2007-07-4.

munity's name changes to South Lake Tahoe, California, and gambling is still illegal.

Prior to 1931, the State Line Country Club was a tiny wayside that featured a small café and a gas pump, but when gambling was legalized, an entrepreneur named Cal Custer purchased the site and converted it into a gambling emporium with a few table games and a handful of slot machines. The club was immediately successful, and in 1933 Custer sold it to business partners Nick Abelman and Steve Pavlovich, who dramatically expanded the facility to include more gambling, a gourmet restaurant, a hardwood dance floor, a huge fireplace, and top-notch entertainment. Pavlovich managed the club until, while gambling in a neighboring casino called the Main Entrance, he accused a dealer of cheating and pulled a gun. Pavlovich was beaten by a bouncer within an inch of his life, and he was seldom seen at the State Line Country Club after that incident. The partners sold the casino in 1945, after which the establishment had several different owners until 1958, when Bill Harrah purchased the property. The Harrah's Lake Tahoe resort now occupies the site.

MINGO, BILL, AND THE CAPTAIN

George Whittell, Jr., and the Thunderbird Lodge

Of all the structures at Lake Tahoe, the prize for most wondrous eccentricity goes to the Thunderbird Lodge, on the lake's eastern shore.

Construction of the lodge began in 1936 under the direction of a delightfully offbeat owner nicknamed "the Captain." George Whittell, Jr., born in 1881, was the pleasure-seeking son of George Sr. and Anna Luning Whittell. Both parents were independently wealthy from banking, mining, and land investments, and when the pair married in 1879, their consolidated fortune was enormous. Shortly after George Jr.'s birth, the Whittells constructed a grandiose mansion on San Francisco's Nob Hill. Raised in pampered comfort, young George defied his parents when he initially refused to attend college and instead joined the Barnum and Bailey Circus. While with the circus he befriended

Flamboyant playboy George Whittell, Jr., and his dog Lever McAwber. Courtesy of the Thunderbird Lodge Preservation Society, Incline Village, Nevada.

Frank Buck, the animal trainer who became world famous as "Bring 'em Back Alive Buck," and together they started an African safari business and made many trips to Africa to capture wild animals for the circus. George Jr. developed a lifelong passion for untamed creatures, especially lions, cheetahs, and elephants.

After a few years, George Jr. left the circus and returned to San Francisco. His parents hoped he would settle down and enter the conservative business arena, and they even arranged a marriage with a respectable debutante, but George Jr. shocked his parents again by eloping with a chorus girl. George Sr. surreptitiously paid county officials to annul the marriage and provided hush money to the bride. The attempted cover-up failed, however, and public scandal erupted in the Whittell's high society. A few years later, George Jr. married Josephine "Josie" Cunningham, a member of a popular vaudeville singing group called the Floradora Sextet, and again his parents strongly objected to the unsuitable match. To punish him, they stopped his considerable allowance, and the combination of his lack of income and his playboy reputation quickly doomed the marriage, although Josie and George Jr. remained lifelong friends.

Following an annulment and restoration of his allowance, George Jr. resumed his self-indulgent lifestyle. One observer stated that his job description consisted of only two words: "millionaire playboy." George Jr. was frequently in the newspapers, often for something outrageous and embarrassing. A 1908 *San Francisco Call* headline read "Son of President of Guatemala Sues for Damages from Being Thrown Downstairs While in Company of George Whittell Jr." In 1919, George Jr. finally married appropriately, in the eyes of his parents. Elia Pascal was a French socialite whose family owned a 1,000-acre estate in France's Loire Valley, a property purchased from the Rockefellers. Although the couple stayed married for the remainder of George Jr.'s life, the union became distant and was kept intact purely as a matter of convenience.

In 1922, George Sr. died, leaving his now forty-year-old son with a $30 million inheritance. Surprising both friends and family, George Jr. managed his finances wisely and his riches grew. In 1929, a few months before the stock market crashed, he sold $50 million worth of stock, thereby weathering the Great Depression with no difficultly and subsequently becoming one of the richest men in America. Also in 1929, Josie presented George Jr. with a pet lion cub. He named the animal Bill and the pair were frequently seen riding in some fine specimen from Whittell's collection of custom automobiles, which included a Duesenberg convertible. Bill would perch comfortably in the front seat, paws on the windshield, his fluffy mane flapping in the breeze.

In the 1930s, Whittell formed a business in Nevada to manage some investments but primarily to avoid California income and estate taxes. While organizing his company, he learned of some property on Lake Tahoe's eastern shore being offered by the Carson and Tahoe Lumber and Flume Company and some other landowners who had been stung by the crash. Whittell would purchase forty thousand acres on the Nevada side of the lake, including more than twenty miles of shoreline—most of Lake Tahoe's eastern rim.

Whittell planned several projects for the property, including real estate developments, ski resorts, a hotel, and a casino, but his first priority was a personal residence, and for that he called up Frederic DeLongchamps, the Nevada State Architect who had built that state's capitol and the Reno Courthouse. DeLongchamps was retained to construct a lakefront estate as well as a boathouse for the Captain's newly commissioned yacht, the opulent *Thunderbird*, a fifty-five-foot wooden vessel designed by John L. Hacker, the preeminent naval architect and motorboat creator of the era. (The *Thunderbird* was commemorated with a US Postal Service stamp in 2007.)

DeLongchamps set to work on six allotted acres. More than one hundred workers labored on the estate buildings for two years. Using native materials wherever possible, they constructed the stone and wood Thunderbird Lodge with two master bedrooms, a great room with a movie theater, servant quarters, and a fully equipped kitchen. The Boathouse, twenty-eight feet wide and one hundred feet long, was the first steel structure erected at Lake Tahoe. The Cook and Butler's House was a one-story residence for the domestic staff. A subterranean Card House was built for high-stakes poker games. The nearby Elephant House looks like a garage, but it was intended to shelter

Whittell's pet elephant, Mingo. There was even a tiny cell called "the Dungeon" to temporarily detain rowdy guests. George Jr. was concerned about security on the opulent domain, and local legend says the property was guarded by wild animals, pack dogs, and former prizefighters. There was also said to have been a sophisticated system that, upon detecting a trespasser, would brightly illuminate the grounds and blare over loudspeakers a recording of the popular song "I'll Be Glad When You're Gone, You Rascal You."

After the Thunderbird Lodge was completed, Whittell became progressively reclusive and spent more and more time at his Lake Tahoe estate. A six-hundred-foot tunnel was built from the lodge to the boathouse to shield him from public view as he walked to his yacht.

By the 1940s, the old Captain spent less time with humans and more time with animals. He brought many of his furry cohorts from his private zoo near San Francisco to keep him company. Mingo the Elephant and Bill the Lion made appearances, as did several trained cheetahs and lions. One summer, a polar bear came to visit. Occasionally, Whittell had guests for all-night poker and drinking sessions, but as he grew older, he increasingly preferred animal companionship.

Following a 1954 mishap, George Jr. was restricted to a wheelchair for the rest of his life. One report stated the confinement was due to a broken leg caused when one of his lions jumped on him and George Jr. refused surgery on his shattered limb. Another account said he was disabled in a shooting accident. He spent his final days at the Thunderbird Lodge and was known to spend hours on end peering into the mesmerizing tranquility of the lake or listening to the sounds of his front porch aviary, an enclosure that held more than forty birds, including six talking mynahs.

George Whittell, Jr., died in 1969 at the age of eighty-seven. Unconventional and glitzy to the end, he insisted upon being buried clad in his favorite ermine coat. Whittell bequeathed large amounts of his fortune to animal rights organizations. The residential and commercial developments originally planned for the Lake Tahoe property were never constructed, and much of the eastern shore remains in a nearly pristine natural condition. Friends and supporters eulogized George

Jr.'s generous spirit. Nevada governor Paul Laxalt, once the Captain's attorney, stated: "Largely through his efforts, much of Nevada's portion of Lake Tahoe is preserved." Others remembered his darker nature and were less generous; upon hearing of his death, one critic dismissed George Jr. as merely a "king-sized playboy with tassels."

Today the lodge property is owned and maintained by the nonprofit Thunderbird Lodge Preservation Society. The Thunderbird Lodge and the George Whittell, Jr., Estate were listed in the National Register of Historic Places in 2000, and much of Whittell's landholdings are now included in the Lake Tahoe, Nevada, State Park, a 14,301-acre recreational area that includes Sand Harbor and Spooner Lake.

Vikingsholm

Imagine: a beautifully handcrafted fairy-tale castle nestled by an ice-cold fjord, ringed with wildflowers and upon a pristine white sand beach. A scene in Norway? No, Lake Tahoe's Emerald Bay. The castle is Vikingsholm, an imaginative reconstruction of a twelfth-century Scandinavian mansion.

Vikingsholm, now part of Emerald Bay State Park, has been open to the public since the 1950s, but its history stretches back to Spring 1928, when heiress Lora Knight purchased the property, which included 239 acres at the west end of Emerald Bay as well as little Fannette Island in the bay. Knight removed the existing structures and began plans for her new "summer cottage."

Struck by Emerald Bay's resemblance to a Scandinavian fjord, Knight decided to build her retreat in a Viking style. The foundation was laid in later summer of 1928, and by fall of 1929, the house was completed. Construction costs exceeded $500,000. Vikingsholm was immediately proclaimed the finest example of Scandinavian architecture in North America—a seamless blending of architectural style and environmental care. Today the home remains preserved as it was built.

Fannette Island in Emerald Bay she had crowned with a small single-room stone Tea House, complete with a miniature fireplace and four tiny windows overlooking the bay. Mrs. Knight and her guests (including such notables as Will Rogers) visited the Tea House frequently, accessing it from the shore via a stairway carved in the native rock. A tea party was a formal occasion calling for the women to wear light summer dresses and carry parasols, and uniformed butlers would grandly row the guests from the mansion to the island for the festivities: tea with lemon, sweet pastries, and witty conversation. However, since there was no restroom on the island, the tea parties tended to be short.

Lora Knight's elaborate mansion Vikingsholm at Emerald Bay, Lake Tahoe, c. 1930. Photograph by Tavern Studio. From the James R. Herz Collection, courtesy of the Special Collections Department, University of Nevada, Reno, UNRS-P1992-01-3290.

THE PHANTOM FOUNTAIN

Thomas Hill

Thomas Hill was an old curmudgeon. One modern-day art critic described him as "an evil-tempered old man sitting like a nineteenth-century spider" in his studio lair at the Wawona Hotel in Yosemite. He started and ended his life in poverty, but at one time he was one of the most successful artistic interpreters of Yosemite Valley.

Hill was born in England in 1829. Showing artistic aptitude at an early age but too poor to afford art supplies, young Hill crafted a brush out of horsehair and began painting when he was seven years old. At the age of fifteen, Hill left England with his family to seek a better life in Massachusetts, and his destitute father put him to work immediately in a cotton mill. A year later, Hill began an apprenticeship with a local carriage painter but ran away soon afterward to join an interior

The interior of painter Thomas Hill's studio at Wawona, Yosemite National Park. Photograph by George Fiske, c. 1880. From "California Views," R. W. Waterman Family Papers, courtesy of The Bancroft Library, University of California, Berkeley, 1905.04360–PIC.

decorating firm in Boston. Still a minor, he had to purchase his freedom from his father to continue with the company.

At the age of twenty-four, Hill studied painting at the Pennsylvania Academy of Fine Art in Philadelphia while supporting himself with part-time work decorating carriages. The next year, in 1854, he advertised himself as a professional artist, specializing in East Coast landscapes. Albert Bierstadt was often Hill's sketching companion on trips to scenic locales, and another colleague, Benjamin Champney, a leading light of the White Mountain School, noted that Hill could "make more pictures in a given time than any other man I have ever met."

But Hill's initial foray into fine art met with failure. In 1859, he returned to decorative art, just scraping by as a painter of flowers and landscapes onto furniture. A year later, he was diagnosed with tuberculosis, and as did many in those days, Hill sought improved health in California, arriving in San Francisco in 1861.

Almost immediately, even as he convalesced, Hill became the kingpin of the tiny cadre of California landscape artists then headquartered in the City by the Bay. It is believed that Hill paid his first visit to Yosemite in 1862, but he did not become artistically active in the valley until a few years later. In 1865, he returned to Yosemite in the company of fellow artist Virgil Williams and photographer Carleton Watkins to consult with landscape architect Frederick Law Olmsted, then a member of the newly established Yosemite Park Commission and already famous as the designer of New York City's Central Park.

The inexhaustible Thomas Hill generated many paintings as a result of this trip, including his 1867 *Yosemite Valley,* which critics quickly noted was not only very realistic but had many similar visual characteristics to an earlier Watkins photograph titled *Up the Valley, Yosemite.* Whereas Albert Bierstadt's detractors had complained about his liberal use of artistic license, Hill's faultfinders protested that he had "essayed large Yosemite views from points which [he had] never visited, but which [his] friend the photographer [Watkins] had." It is possible that Hill may have consulted Watkins's image while completing the painting in Paris, during a period of study in France.

Despite a recurrence of health problems, Hill was gaining notice in the art world and was active in the art market. His Yosemite paintings were publicly exhibited to widespread favorable response in Boston and were reproduced as lithographs by publisher Louis Prang. Several compositions were purchased by *nouveau riche* California railroad tycoons, entrepreneurs, and financiers to decorate their salons. Railroad mogul and politician Leland Stanford bought Hill's 1876 oil *Yosemite Valley* for his Nob Hill mansion, and brothers Edwin and Charles Crocker, of the Central Pacific Railroad, purchased two canvases in 1872 for $15,000. William Ralston, founder of the Bank of California, exhibited Hill's landscapes in the bank's lobby, and the developers of San Francisco's ornate Palace Hotel acquired a Hill composition for display in the hotel.

Seemingly overnight, the struggling artist was wealthy and in demand. Hill's work was exhibited to acclaim in New York City and San Francisco, and he was awarded the "Best in Landscape" prize at Philadelphia's Centennial International Exposition of 1876, the first World's Fair. Buyers were abundant, particularly in California, and Hill dominated the market for Yosemite scenes.

In 1877, Hill accepted a commission from Leland Stanford to produce a colossal commemoration of the May 10, 1869, ceremony at Promontory Point, Utah, that marked the completion of the Transcontinental Railroad. The painting would feature the likenesses of nearly four hundred individuals who participated in the event. Stanford personally supervised the composition and made frequent demands for alterations, mostly in the arrangement of figures in the painting. In 1879, when Hill had partially completed the massive work, an economic recession rocked California and the market for paintings declined. Hill put his entire energy behind the completion of Stanford's commission as his other sales withered. By 1880, San Francisco insiders reported that "Thomas Hill has not sold a picture in eight months."

After three years, Stanford's painting, entitled *The Last Spike*, was nearly finished. Charles Crocker, one of the Big Four and the construction head of the Central Pacific Railroad, visited Hill and was outraged that Stanford had ordered Hill to move Crocker's figure to a less prominent position in the painting. Crocker was especially angry that Stanford himself was the central figure in the painting, and he stormed out, exclaiming loudly,

"What damn nonsense is that?!" When the eight-by-twelve-foot canvas was finally completed, Stanford was no longer interested in its purchase. The two never spoken again, and Hill was never able to sell the painting. For many years, *The Last Spike* hung in the rotunda of the California State Capitol, but today the painting is prominently displayed at the California State Railroad Museum in Sacramento.

Having put all of his hopes into this commission, Hill was desperate for cash and his health began to deteriorate. The extraordinarily prolific artist had produced hundreds of canvases, which he then attempted to sell at auction. The auctioneer, realizing that sales would be slow, helpfully suggested to the crowd that the paintings would appreciate upon Hill's death, which appeared to be imminent. Still, the auctioned paintings went for low prices and Hill went on to live for another twenty-five years.

Now in his fifties, Hill turned his attention away from monumental canvases toward the tourist trade in Yosemite. He established a studio at the Wawona Hotel at Yosemite's southern entrance in 1883 and scraped by selling his paintings to park visitors. He produced a huge catalog of souvenir keepsake landscapes during this period, but collectors and critics regarded his work as increasingly outdated and sloppy. Former customers abandoned him, and Hill's daughter often had to physically steer potential customers into the studio and art gallery.

In 1885, Hill painted *The Wawona Hotel*, an oil that depicted the exterior of the resort and Hill's studio. In a flight of whimsy, he included a fountain in front of the hotel where in reality only a lawn existed. After the image was included in James Mason Hutchings's 1886 book *The Heart of the Sierras*, hotel visitors would arrive at the location disappointed to find that in fact there was no fountain. In response, the proprietors added one in 1889, and it still exists today.

In 1896, Hill suffered the first of several strokes. He never fully recovered and painted few canvases after that. A final moment of glory occurred in May 1903, when President Theodore Roosevelt visited Hill's studio while on a tour of Yosemite. Roosevelt admired a large painting of Bridal Veil Fall, which Hill presented to him as a gift. Hill learned soon afterward that Roosevelt, a prodigious art collector, had acquired nearly his entire collection as a result of similar generosity.

In 1908, Thomas Hill died at the age of eighty in the village of Raymond, about forty miles southwest of Yosemite. He could no longer paint, and many speculated that he committed suicide.

SIERRA SPOTLIGHT

Thomas Moran

Thomas Moran was perhaps the most widely known and respected landscape painter of the nineteenth century. And Yosemite was always on his mind.

Born in England in 1837, Moran relocated to the United States as a young boy. As he grew to adulthood in New York, his skills as an artist blossomed and it quickly became evident that he was a superb illustrator and an impeccable painter with a flair for color.

Moran first traveled West in 1871, at the invitation of the United States Geological Survey, conducted by Ferdinand von Hayden. Moran was captivated by the grandeur of the American West and understood the emotional importance of representing a vision of the landscape rather than simply a reproduction.

While best known for his monumental depictions of Yellowstone, Moran particularly loved Yosemite. He first visited the valley in 1872, and his body of work included dozens of paintings and illustrations of the magnificent park. His engraving of Half Dome is one of the best known published images of Yosemite from the period, and the vantage point he utilized was later named Moran Point in his honor. Moran visited Yosemite on only four occasions, but the memories were indelible. Upon his death the vast majority of his collection was donated to the National Park Service and displayed in Yosemite.

When Thomas Moran died in 1926, at age eighty-nine, an unfinished piece rested on his easel. It was a painting of Yosemite's Bridal Veil Fall.

Portrait of the influential artist and illustrator Thomas Moran. Photograph by Napoleon Sarony, c. 1895. Courtesy of the Library of Congress, Prints and Photographs Division, Washington, DC, LC-USZ62-115323.

THE LITTLE TRAMP IN TRUCKEE

Charlie Chaplin and The Gold Rush

Charlie Chaplin's *Gold Rush* is considered by many to be one of the best and most influential films ever made. Chaplin himself referred to it as "the picture that I want to be remembered by." The famous scenes of the Little Tramp eating a boiled shoe, battling with a teetering cabin seesawing on the edge of a cliff, and performing a remarkable dance using two forks stuck into bread rolls remain among cinema's most indelible images.

By 1924, Charlie Chaplin was the most famous entertainer in the world and, quite probably, the most famous person in the world. He was also the highest paid actor. In 1916, his contract called for a paycheck

A young Charles Chaplin at the beginning of his worldwide celebrity, c. 1920. By the time his film *The Gold Rush* was produced in 1925, Chaplin was the most famous person in the world. From the George Grantham Bain Collection, courtesy of the Library of Congress, Prints and Photographs Division, Washington, DC, LC-DIG-ggbain-21143.

of $10,000 per week (in today's purchasing power that would be about $175,000 weekly), and by 1924, with his popularity at its zenith, no studio could afford him. Along with partners Douglas Fairbanks and Mary Pickford, another two of the most popular film stars of the era, Chaplin founded United Artists in 1919 to independently make and distribute films. The distribution contract called for Chaplin to receive 50 percent of the profits from his movies and retain copyrights after a few years.

Chaplin was fascinated with the story of the Donner Party and endeavored to make a movie that explored enduring great hardships in pursuit of a better life. He chose Alaska's 1898 Yukon gold rush as his setting.

Chaplin's *Gold Rush* followed his usual pattern of production: there was a basic outline of the story but no actual script. Chaplin had used this method for years, building a film from a mixture of a skeletal story and constant experimentation and retakes. He used only one camera and produced more than 230,000 feet of film, which together totaled almost forty-three hours. The final product was an hour and a half long, had taken seventeen months to complete, and cost $923,886, making it the most expensive comedy of the entire silent-film era.

The Gold Rush was revolutionary in that it used film comedy to explore an actual historical event. Chaplin decided to enhance the authenticity by filming on location, a concept that was not new but that Chaplin pushed to an unprecedented scope. Truckee was chosen as the ideal setting to recreate Chilkoot Pass, the famous trail that led into the Yukon, and Chaplin intended to film all of the exterior scenes exclusively in the Sierra town.

Truckee was no stranger to the motion picture industry and had been used a number of times for outdoor scenes by the famous film comedian Buster Keaton. Chaplin and Keaton were close friends and Chaplin was well aware of Truckee's desirability as a shooting location. Also, given his interest in the Donner Party, it is not surprising Truckee was his choice. Filming began in February 1924 and lasted until April 28 of that year.

Chaplin restaged the snow-covered Chilkoot Pass for the film's opening sequence, a scene that shows hundreds of desperate miners struggling to climb the steep, narrow path that reaches through the pass and to the Yukon Territory. Summit Mountain, in today's Sugar Bowl Ski Resort, was the location, and the Truckee Ski Club cleared the path for the single-file trail of actors, which included six hundred men brought from Sacramento by train to serve as extras. The scene was shot entirely in one day and remains what film critic Jeffrey Vance calls "the most spectacular image of silent-film comedy."

Chaplin had planned to film extensively in Truckee, and he and his crew set up residence in the Summit Hotel at Donner Pass and the Swedish House Hotel downtown. When the winter weather turned nasty and many crew members and extras came down with colds—Chaplin himself contracted influenza—they decided to suspend filming in Truckee and concentrate on using controllable (and undoubtedly warmer) studio sets. Even after struggling through difficult conditions and exposing thousands of feet of film, much of the Truckee footage ended up on the cutting room floor. The final version of the film includes only two parts shot in Truckee: the Chilkoot Pass sequence and a scene in which the Little Tramp slides down a snowy slope.

Production work on *The Gold Rush* was completed in May 1925, and on June 26 of that year the film was lavishly premiered at Hollywood's Egyptian Theatre. The theater owner, Sid Grauman (who would become renowned as the owner of Grauman's Chinese Theatre, where movie star shoe- and handprints are permanently displayed in the concrete sidewalks) was a former goldseeker himself and had in fact traveled to Truckee to serve as an advisor on the set.

The film opened to wide acclaim—and great profit. *The Gold Rush* grossed $6 million and was without doubt the most profitable film comedy of the silent-movie era.

SIERRA SPOTLIGHT

Greed

The first full-length feature film made in the Sierra Nevada was a monumental effort and remains an ongoing Hollywood legend. Produced in 1924, *Greed* was nearly ten hours long in its original form. A silent-film landmark, it was a faithful adaptation of the novel *McTeague,* by Frank Norris. Scenes were filmed in Oakland, San Francisco, Death Valley, and Placer County.

Directed by the eccentric and demanding Eric von Stroheim, the film cost $500,000 to produce—an astounding amount for the time. Von Stroheim was insistent that the film capture every detail and nuance of its source material—a demand that accounted for its exaggerated length—but it was shown only once in its entirety, and only to meet contractual obligations. *Greed* was then cut, and cut again, by a studio employee until it was only two and a half hours long. Even then, the film was a financial failure.

Most of the edited film was accidentally destroyed by a janitor, who tossed what he thought was unimportant celluloid strips into an incinerator. As a result, *Greed* is considered one of the great "lost films" of cinema. Although a full-length restoration is impossible, Turner Entertainment, which holds the rights to the film, recently fashioned a version of the movie under the direction of film archivist Rick Schmidlin. Schmidlin pieced together existing footage and more than six hundred production stills to create an approximation of Von Stroheim's movie. The new version was still about six hours shorter than the original.

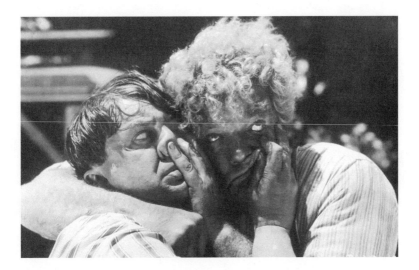

A production still from *Greed,* Erich von Stroheim's 1924 silent film epic and the first feature film made in the Sierra Nevada. The two actors are Jean Hersholt and Gibson Gowland. Courtesy of The Bancroft Library, University of California, Berkeley, 1993.034:31–fALB.

REEL-LIFE EXPERIENCE

Railtown and the Alabama Hills

From as early as Hollywood became a movie town, the Sierra Nevada has been the production venue for hundreds of films, television programs, and commercials. Granted, the range is relatively close to the Southern California entertainment hub, but surely the Sierra's diverse topography and breathtaking beauty were enticements in and of themselves.

Occasionally, Sierra Nevada reel and real life intertwine in curious ways. In *The Godfather II* (1974), perhaps the most startling and disturbing scene is when mafia chieftan Michael Corleone has his brother, the slow-witted Fredo, murdered for betraying the Family. The execution occurs in a fishing boat in the middle of Lake Tahoe; Fredo is shot in the head and his body is wrapped in chains and dumped overboard.

Cowboy movie star Ken Maynard and a film production crew, c. 1930. Maynard filmed many of his Western movies in the Alabama Hills of Inyo County. From the Anthony Amaral Collection, courtesy of the Special Collections Department, University of Nevada, Reno, UNRS-P1983-03-046.

The visual impact of the scene—of the clear blue waters, the stormy sky full of malevolent clouds, and the brutal fratricide—are a combination so unforgettable and real that, to this day, some tourists wonder aloud whether Fredo's body has ever resurfaced.

Lake Tahoe played itself in *The Godfather II,* but other Sierra locations have been filmed to look like places all over the world—both real and fictional. In the diversity of the range, directors have found slices of, among other locales, New York, Dodge City, Coffeeville, Denver, Virginia City, Hooterville, Thailand, Venezuela, Camp David, Austria, New England, Montana, Canada, the Melody Ranch, the Ponderosa Ranch, India, Afghanistan, Spain during the Roman Empire, the planet Veridian III, Africa, China, the Yukon, Alabama, and even dinosaur-infested territory during the Jurassic era. Beverly Lewis, director of the Placer–Lake Tahoe Film Office, once recalled having two major films in simultaneous production only one mile apart in the county yet a world away from each other. One movie was set in Venezuela, the other in Alaska.

Greed, the first feature film made in the Sierra, was produced in 1924, but the range had been used for shorter films as early as 1915. Every Sierra Nevada county has been used for Hollywood motion pictures, but two filming locations are especially beloved: Railtown in Tuolumne County, and the Alabama Hills, near Lone Pine in Inyo County.

Railtown 1897 State Historic Park, located in Jamestown, is a steam-powered valentine to the railroad and to Hollywood. The twenty-six-acre park is the home of the roundhouse and shops for the Sierra Railway, a functioning line that has been in business since 1897 and still services regional lumber companies by transporting rock, gravel, and wood chips. The Sierra Railway provided building materials for the string of dams constructed along the Stanislaus and Tuolumne Rivers in the mid-twentieth century. In 1982, the Sierra Railway site was purchased by the state for use as an historic park.

The Sierra Railway has also been featured in hundreds of motion pictures, television productions, and commercials, beginning with its first appearance in a cliffhanging eighteen-episode silent-movie serial entitled *The Red Glove* (1919). Subsequently, Railtown provided the location for many films, including *The Virginian* (1929), *Dodge City* (1939), *Young Thomas Edison* (1940), *Go West* (1940), *Duel in the Sun* (1947), *High Noon* (1952), *Bound for Glory* (1976), *Back to the Future III* (1990), and *Unforgiven* (1992, and the Academy Award recipient for Best Picture). Television shows such as *Gunsmoke, Bonanza, The Wild, Wild West,* and *Little House on the Prairie* all used Railtown. The yard's most famous steam engine, Locomotive No. 3, was itself a popular TV star as the Hooterville Cannonball on *Petticoat Junction.*

South of Railtown is a location practically everyone has seen on TV—and maybe as recently as last night. The Alabama Hills, managed by the US Bureau of Land Management as protected habitat and for public enjoyment, is a range of hills and rock formations adjacent to the eastern escarpment of the Sierra Nevada, west of Lone Pine. The landscape is bizarre and striking; the collection of weathered lumps—orange volcanic rock and gray granitic rock—rest in the shadow of Mount Whitney, the tallest mountain in the lower forty-eight states. The area also features dozens of wind-carved natural arches with mysterious names like Mobius Arch, Lathe Arch, the Eye of Alabama, and Whitney Portal Arch.

The Alabama Hills were named for the Confederate war sloop the CSS *Alabama,* known for lightning-quick strikes and amazing seamanship. When news of the ship's exploits reached residents in California, quite a few of whom were sympathetic to the Confederate cause, they named many mining claims near Lone Pine after the ship, and the label eventually came to be applied to the entire area.

Since the silent-movie days, the Alabama Hills have been a popular filming location for television and film—especially Westerns, and particularly shoot-'em-up scenes. Among the Alabama Hills' long list of credits are the Tom Mix films, the Hopalong Cassidy films, *The Gene Autry Show* (and its Melody Ranch), *The Lone Ranger, Under Western Stars* (1938, featuring Roy Rogers in his first starring role), *Gunga Din* (1939, with the Alabama Hills doubling for the Khyber Pass), *The Ox-Bow Incident* (1941), *Springfield Rifle* (1952), *The Violent Men* (1955), *Bad Day at Black Rock* (1955), *How the West Was Won* (1962), *The Great Race* (1965), and *Joe Kidd* (1972). More recently, automobile manufacturers have used the roughhewn landscape for dozens of car commercials, most notably Dodge's "Ram Tough" truck ads.

Since the 1990s, the Alabama Hills have been featured in many profitable and a few blockbuster-sized movies. *Star Trek VII: Generations* (1994) saw Captains Kirk and Picard on the planet Veridian III— actually the Alabama Hills—in the same year the comedic Western *Maverick* prominently featured the unique topography. In 2000, Disney used background plates of the location for its computer-animated film *Dinosaur*, and in 2008, the hills became Afghanistan in *Iron Man*, which was produced by Marvel Studios, a subsidiary of Disney. In 2012, director Quentin Tarantino's Oscar-nominated *Django Unchained* was partially filmed in the remarkable setting.

Perhaps one of the most dramatic uses of the Alabama Hills was in the Academy Award–winning epic *Gladiator* (2000). In one extraordinary scene, the bloodied gladiator played by Russell Crowe has escaped from his Roman Imperial captors and is furiously galloping his horse toward his home in second-century Spain. In the background are California's Alabama Hills and Mount Whitney.

SIERRA SPOTLIGHT

The Sierra Nevada as Somewhere Else

Railtown and the Alabama Hills might receive the majority of the attention and acclaim, but every county in the Sierra Nevada has been used as a location for at least one feature film.

Does the Sierra remind you of Maryland? It did for the producers of *The American President* (1995), who used the mountains in El Dorado County to depict the Camp David presidential retreat. How about the Sierra as New England? It passed in *A Place in the Sun* (1951). Got a hankering to visit Canada? Hollywood took a shortcut when it used Lake Tahoe's Emerald Bay to depict Quebec in *Rose Marie* (1936). Ever thought the Sierra Nevada had a tropical feel? The production teams of three films thought so: *Anna and the King* (1999) used the mountains for Thailand, *George of the Jungle* (1997) used Placer County for

Africa, and *Dragonfly* (2001) used the American River as a waterway in Venezuela. *True Lies* (1999), starring future California governor Arnold Scharwzenegger, substituted a ski area near Lake Tahoe for a resort near Washington, DC, and speaking of governors, the Wilson-McConnell House, a former governor's mansion in Columbia State Historic Park, was used as the New Mexico home of Gary Cooper's character in *High Noon* (1952). Thanks to a bit of fancy footwork that would make Hollywood proud, the house, which was not actually a governor's mansion, was given the distinction for one day only, as part of the 1945 ceremony dedicating the establishment of the state's newest historic park.

The Sierra Nevada standing in for the Canadian wilderness in a 1925 silent film. The location is Emerald Lake in Sequoia National Park. From the Francis Farquhar Collection, courtesy of The Bancroft Library, University of California, Berkeley, 1954.008—PIC Box 3 Series II–Sequoia.

SOUL-
CONSOLING
TOWER

Manzanar

At the base of towering, snow-veined Mount Williamson, a desert basin is scolded by gusts and dusty whirlwinds. This expanse of eastern Sierra is lonely but alive with color: the greenish yellow of blooming sage, the granite-gray and white-capped peaks, the blue ribbons of icy streams, the pink lace of winter willows, and the brown of weathered wooden fence posts. Standing starkly on the horizon is a solitary white obelisk carved with jet black Japanese characters that translate to "Soul-Consoling Tower." It is a haunting and sobering reminder that this was the site of Manzanar, a World War II concentration camp where more

A fire crew knocks down dust at Manzanar, a World War II–era internment camp for Japanese Americans in the eastern Sierra Nevada. Photograph by Dorothea Lange, July 2, 1942. From War Relocation Authority (WRA) Photographs, series 8, volume 23, section C, WRA-no. C-880, 1967.014 v. 42:12EH-149—PIC, courtesy of The Bancroft Library, University of California, Berkeley.

than eleven thousand Japanese and Japanese Americans were imprisoned simply because they looked like the enemy.

Following the December 7, 1941, Imperial Japanese attack on Pearl Harbor that thrust the United States into World War II, the United States government moved aggressively to curtail threats and subversive activities by people of Japanese ancestry. Their bank accounts were frozen, they were given a mandatory curfew, they were required to carry identification papers, and they were subject to home raids and property seizures by FBI and Treasury agents who did not have to produce search warrants. Ida Nishiguchi witnessed the degrading aftereffects of Pearl Harbor as a young girl, starting when her father, an employee of the Western Pacific Railroad Company, was abruptly fired following the attack. He was falsely considered a saboteur, and the innocent family was given twenty-four hours to vacate railroad property, after which they were still constantly followed by government and railroad agents. Ida's sister was even accompanied to her high school graduation ceremony by an armed constable.

On February 19, 1942, President Franklin Roosevelt signed Executive Order 9066, which authorized the construction of a string of inland "relocation centers" to house the forced resettlement of over one hundred twenty thousand Japanese and Japanese Americans, two-thirds of whom were native-born American citizens. The internment order required all Japanese and Japanese Americans to secure or sell their property and report to "assembly centers" while permanent internment camps were being constructed. There were sixteen assembly centers in all, including thirteen in California. Internees were restricted from taking with them to the camp items not considered "essential personal effects," and the order also noted that "the size and number of packages is limited to that which can be carried by the individual or family group."

Within weeks, thousands of men, women, and children were forced to dispose of their property and journey by bus and train to the camps, not knowing when—or if—they would be allowed to return to their homes. Tamiko Sugioka Hata, seventeen years old in 1942, remembered her trip to the assembly center: "There was a [railroad] tunnel [near Penryn, Placer County]....We went there [by bus] and then we went up the hill and then one of the friends said, 'Now, Grandpa, look back, this is the last time for you to see your home.'" Amy Uyeda of Placer County recalled her train ride to the Fresno Assembly Center: "We had to pull the curtains down in the train and we didn't know why, but we were told that if we pulled the curtains up and looked out the window, we'd be shot at."

Manzanar was the first of what ultimately amounted to ten concentration camps stretching from California to Arkansas. In 1942, the US Army leased 6,200 acres at Manzanar from the City of Los Angeles— the city had acquired the land during the Owens Valley water wars of the early 1900s—but only 540 acres were developed for the camp and the rest was a wide expanse of desert at the foot of the Sierra. The residential area was about one square mile and consisted of thirty-six blocks of tarpaper barracks. Each barracks building was twenty feet wide and one hundred feet long, and each imprisoned family was given an "apartment" within the structure. The living quarters had almost no privacy, as each apartment was separated only by flimsy partitions that didn't reach to the ceilings. Manzanar housed 11,070 prisoners in total.

In her 1973 memoir *Farewell to Manzanar*, Jeanne Wakatsuki Houston, who was only seven years old at the time of internment, describes her arrival to the camp and her barracks:

> After dinner we were taken to Block 16, a cluster of fifteen
> barracks that had just been finished a day or so earlier—
> although finished was hardly the word for it. The shacks
> were built of one thickness of pine planking covered with
> tarpaper. They sat on concrete footings, with about two
> feet of open space between the floorboards and the ground.
> Gaps showed between the planks, and as the weeks passed
> and the green wood dried out, the gaps widened. Knot-
> holes gaped in the uncovered floor....We were issued
> steel army cots, two brown army blankets each, and some
> mattress covers, which my brothers stuffed with straw.

Each residential block had a communal mess hall, a laundry room, a recreation hall (except Block 33), an ironing room, and a heating-oil storage tank. The camp had schools, an auditorium, chicken and hog farms, churches, a cemetery, a post office, a co-op store, and a camp newspaper.

The camps were advertised as providing protection for the Japanese American population, yet they were built not like forts but prisons. Manzanar's perimeter featured eight watchtowers manned by armed military police, and the entire facility was enclosed by barbed wire. As one detainee famously stated, "If the camp was built to protect us, why were the machine guns facing in?"

With the conclusion of World War II in May 1945, the War Relocation Authority began the process of closing Manzanar and the other camps. Each prisoner was given twenty-five dollars, one-way train or bus fare, and, occasionally, funds for meals. Many left the camps immediately, but a sizeable number refused to leave until forced, as they did not have anything to return to. While there were some instances of Japanese Americans returning home to find that sympathetic neighbors had safeguarded their property and belongings, many were faced with homesteads in disrepair and communities full of hostility. When Frank Kageta, a decorated veteran of the 442nd Regimental Combat Team, headed home to Loomis, in Placer County, he believed his family's possessions had been placed in safekeeping. Upon arrival, however, he discovered the items had disappeared and that signs exclaiming "No Japs Allowed!" were posted throughout his hometown.

Sometimes there was also violence. In 1945, Sumio Doi and his Auburn family were the first to return to Placer County following internment. The family fruit farm was in poor condition after three years of neglect, but that was only the beginning of their troubles. A few days after his arrival, Doi was relaxing in his house when he heard cars in the farmyard. Surprised, he went to investigate and saw his packing shed ablaze. He managed to snuff out the flames, and did not alert the authorities, but two days later, in the dark of night, the cars returned. When Doi opened the door to investigate, shots were fired into the house. Doi immediately reported the attack to the police, and when a patrol car of deputies arrived, they saw two cars speeding away. The suspects escaped, but they left evidence behind. Carefully placed under one corner of the packing shed were several sticks of dynamite. The fuses had been lit but had burned out.

Several days later, seven people were arrested for the incidents and they were put on trial. The defendants had given confessions and the defense offered no denial of their statements, but they all formally pled not guilty. The defendants were not called to testify and were not cross-examined, and the defense offered no witnesses on their behalf. It appeared to be an open and shut case. In the end, the jury acquitted the suspects and their legal fees were paid by contributions collected from local residents in donations ranging from fifty cents to one hundred dollars.

At Manzanar after the war, all but a handful of the structures were leveled and the site returned to its more-or-less natural state. Today there are markers delineating barrack foundations and other infrastructure, remnants of internee landscaping, and the restored Manzanar Camp High School Auditorium, which houses a museum. The location is a California Historical Landmark and a National Historic Site, and the land itself is now owned by the National Park Service.

The brazen incarceration of more than one hundred ten thousand people without trial and in the absence of any crime constitutes one of the darkest chapters in American history.

SIERRA SPOTLIGHT

The 442nd Regimental Combat Team

While their families were incarcerated in internment camps throughout the United States, thousands of young Japanese American men were fighting and dying for their country during World War II. The 442nd Regimental Combat Team's record was unmatched in its time, and it remains the most decorated infantry regiment of its size and length of service in American history.

Made up of volunteers, the 442nd fought primarily in Europe. Its members served with exceptional bravery and valor, and the list of their awards and commendations is breathtaking. In all, fourteen thousand soldiers served in the 442nd, and the overall casualty rate—which includes those killed, missing, and wounded—was an unusually high 93 percent. The 442nd earned 9,486 Purple Hearts and the unit received an unparalleled 8 Presidential Unit Citations. Individual soldiers were awarded 21 Medals of Honor, 52 Distinguished Service Crosses, 560 Silver Stars (with 28 Oak Leaf Clusters, signifying a second award), and 4,000 Bronze Stars (with 1,200 Oak Leaf Clusters).

In October 2010, the Congressional Gold Medal was awarded to the surviving members of the 442nd Regimental Combat Team.

The all–Japanese American 442nd Regimental Combat Team training at Camp Shelby, Mississippi. This highly decorated unit fought with great distinction in Europe during World War II. From War Relocation Authority (WRA) Photographs, series 12, Relocation, vol. 43, section E, WRA H-164, courtesy of The Bancroft Library, University of California, Berkeley.

BEHOLD THE WANDERING MOON

The Wakamatsu Tea and Silk Colony

In June 1869, a dogged group of travelers arrived near Coloma. Among the party were a Prussian attaché and his family, a handful of Japanese samurai, and a teenager named Okei Ito. In their possession were mulberry trees, tea plant seeds, fruit tree saplings, paper and oil plants, rice, bamboo, and other crops they had brought from their Japanese homeland. With these items and an abundance of anticipation, this vanguard established the Wakamatsu Tea and Silk Colony, believed to be the first permanent Japanese settlement in North America. The

The gravesite of Okei Ito at the Wakamatsu Tea and Silk Colony, El Dorado County. Founded in 1869, the Wakamatsu colony is believed to have been the first permanent Japanese settlement in North America. Photograph taken in 1969, on the one hundredth anniversary of the colony. Courtesy of the Japanese American Archival Collection, Department of Special Collections and University Archives, The Library, California State University, Sacramento, no. JC17A:20.

colony was the birthplace of the first naturalized Japanese American citizen and the only settlement established by samurai outside of Japan.

The colony had its origin in centuries-old domestic Japanese politics. In the seventeenth century, the Tokugawa shogunate, the feudal political structure that ruled the island from 1603 to 1868, adopted as its keystone policies cultural isolation and prohibitions on foreign travel. These policies reigned supreme for two hundred fifty years, until Commodore Matthew Perry of the United States Navy established trade with Japanese ports in 1853 and 1854, primarily through military intimidation. Perry's foray opened the door to foreign cultural intrusion, and by the 1860s the shogunate's traditional seclusion was crumbling. The Tokugawa leadership attempted to stem the tide, but a local *daimyo*, or lord, of the Aizu Wakamatsu Province publicly disagreed with shogunate policy and felt that some form of cooperation with the Westerners was a more prudent course. His name was Matsudaira Katamori.

Katamori was friendly with the European diplomat John Henry Schnell, who was attached to the Prussian Embassy. Schnell sold European-style weaponry, and Katamori was one of his best customers. Schnell trained samurai in the use of European firearms and achieved great respect in his adopted community: he was awarded a Japanese name, allowed to marry a Japanese samurai-class woman, and given the rank of General.

Changes to Japanese society following Commodore Perry's arrival led to bitter discord between the Tokugawa faction (including the disaffected Katamori) and its enemies, who wished for the restoration of the Imperial monarchy. The result was the bloody Boshin Civil War of 1868–1869, a conflict also known as the War of the Year of the Dragon. In 1868, Katamori's force of four thousand samurai was roundly defeated by the emperor's army of twenty thousand soldiers at Aizu, in Wakamatsu Province. Katamori surrendered and was sentenced to execution, and his friend and supporter Schnell suddenly found his own life in danger.

In April 1869, with Katamori's financial support, Schnell arranged for a steam-powered clipper ship, the SS *China*, to carry some Wakamatsu refugees to the United States. Among the passengers were Schnell's Japanese wife, Jou; their daughter Frances; some of Katamori's veteran samurai; and the seventeen-year-old Okei, the Schnell family's nursemaid.

Arriving in San Francisco on May 20, 1869, the refugees were an exotic novelty. The San Francisco *Daily Alta California* gushed over Jou's beauty as well as the company's cargo, which included fifty thousand mulberry trees (to be used for silk cultivation), six million tea seeds, and countless silkworm cocoons. The new arrivals also brought cooking utensils, swords, and a large banner bearing the Aizu Wakamatsu lotus blossom crest.

Within weeks, the colonists, under the direction of Schnell, purchased two hundred acres and outbuildings in Gold Hill, one mile from Coloma, and began the daunting task of establishing a profitable agricultural colony. They planted mulberry trees and tea seeds, cultivated other crops (most notably citrus, peaches, and other stone fruits), and built dwellings. In January 1870, a correspondent for the San Francisco *Morning Call* traveled to the tea and silk colony and reported on the progress, commenting favorably on Japanese ingenuity, neatness, intellect, and manners: "The men are bright, intelligent, and polite, lifting their hats and bowing gracefully to strangers, and the women stay at home, do the cooking, take care of the babies, keep the house in order, and manage pretty much as American housewives do."

The Wakamatsu Tea and Silk Colony flourished for a while. The colonists proudly displayed their products at the 1869 California State Agricultural Fair in Sacramento and the 1870 Horticultural Fair in San Francisco. But the colony faltered when faced with a prolonged drought, increased water costs and competition, and, most importantly, the withdrawal of funding from Katamori. In 1869, the Boshin War ended in defeat for the Tokugawa shogunate and brought about the Meiji Restoration, or the reinstallation of Imperial dynastic control. Katamori, sentenced to death during the war by the now victorious Meiji leadership, was surprisingly pardoned and chose to remain in Japan as a Shinto priest. In his new personal and professional circumstances, Katamori discontinued funding to the colony.

In 1873, the Francis Veerkamp Family purchased the Wakamatsu lands and the colony was disbanded, although several of the settlers remained on the property, including Matsunosoke Sakurai, who worked for the Veerkamps until his death in 1901. The fates of only a few of the colonists are known, but among them is Masumizu Kuninosuke, who married Carrie Wilson, an African and Native American woman from Coloma, and whose descendants still live in the region.

And what of Okei Ito, the seventeen-year-old nursemaid of the Schnell family? Profoundly homesick and lonely, it is said that Okei would walk each evening to the highest point of the colony, gaze longingly westward while dreaming of her home, and sing tearful lullabies. She fervently hoped that Schnell would somehow repatriate her to Japan. It did not happen. Okei contracted a fever and died in 1871, only nineteen years old. She is buried on the former Wakamatsu Colony property, under a tree on the hill she visited each night.

But the story does not end there. In the early 1920s, Japanese Americans began tending to Okei's grave and emphasizing the importance of the Wakamatsu Colony in the history of Japanese immigration to the United States. Following the end of the Boshin Civil War and the Meiji Restoration, rapid modernization and social upheaval rocked Japan, and many Japanese hopefuls wished to start afresh in new lands. They looked to the Wakamatsu experiment as a model for immigration that preserved cultural cohesion, and still today the Wakamatsu Tea and Silk Colony is widely regarded as the beginning of permanent US settlement by what came to be known as the Issei (first-generation Japanese Americans). By 1900, more than twenty thousand Japanese and Japanese Americans were living in the United States, and an estimated 10 percent of all California agricultural production was credited to Japanese settlers.

Okei Ito was the first Japanese person buried on American soil, and in recent years her gravesite has become a pilgrimage destination. In 1969, then California governor Ronald Reagan designated the Wakamatsu Colony site as California Historic Landmark #815, and in 1969, on the one hundredth anniversary of the colony, Japanese American community leaders proclaimed the year as the Japanese American Centennial. A commemorative ceremony at the Wakamatsu Colony featured official representation by Japanese Consul General Shima Seichi and a visit from Matsudaira Ichiro, the grandson of colony financier Matsudaira Katamori.

In November 2010, the American River Conservancy purchased the 272-acre Gold Hill–Wakamatsu Tea and Silk Colony Farm with plans to preserve, protect, and interpret the location's social history and cultural legacy. Sacramento congressional representative Doris Matsui stated that "to many Japanese Americans, the Wakamatsu Colony is as symbolic as Plymouth Rock was for the first American colonists."

SIERRA SPOTLIGHT

Burnette Haskell and the Kaweah Colony

In 1886, a fascinating assembly of idealists was heading toward a spectacular grove of giant sequoias to embark on an innovative social experiment. Their leader was Burnette Haskell, a San Francisco lawyer, publisher, and union organizer. Influenced by utopian socialism, Haskell and his followers founded the Cooperative Land Purchase and Colonization Association near the Kaweah River in the southern Sierra. The Kaweah Co-Operative Commonwealth had about three hundred residents, and it was their communal society that garnered the most attention. Kaweah Colony organized its economy on a "time check" system that would pay for the amount of work performed and could only be redeemed at the colony store. If you worked 200 minutes, you would receive a "time check" worth one dollar. Denominations ranged from 10 to 100,000 minutes, women received equal pay for equal work, and all work was considered identical in value. Health care in the colony was free.

In 1892, riven by internal dissension, the Kaweah Colony collapsed. Burnette Haskell returned to San Francisco, where he died in 1907 in a dilapidated shack, embittered and drug-addled.

Burnett Haskell, leader of the short-lived utopian Kaweah Colony, Tulare County. Photograph by Thors, December 1880. From the California Faces Collection, courtesy of The Bancroft Library, University of California, Berkeley, G.–POR 110.

STOVELEG
PITONS AND
CHEAP RED WINE

Warren Harding and El Capitan

The 1930s was an especially rewarding time for Yosemite climbers. In the summer of 1930, Robert Underhill returned from two years climbing in the Alps ready to share his newfound knowledge of European rope techniques with Francis Farquhar, an avid mountaineer and the editor of the *Sierra Club Bulletin*. Farquhar asked Underhill to write an article for the *Bulletin* describing the new procedures, and in February 1931, Underhill's twenty-page article was published, piquing the interest of a brave little band of rock climbers known as the Sierra Club.

The San Francisco–based group organized outings that used Underhill's rope techniques and other European methods, such as the running belay and Dülfersitz rappel, and by the summer of that same

Rock climber Warren Harding on the Nose of El Capitan during the first ascent of the Yosemite Valley granite monolith in 1957. From a Bill "Dolt" Feuerer Proofsheet, courtesy of the Yosemite Climbing Association, Yosemite, California.

year, the climbers were making their first Sierra ascents, including on a new route to the summit of Mount Whitney using this latest *modus operandi*. The only items they lacked were the carefully engineered and expensive rock pitons then being used in Europe. A piton is essentially an iron peg with a circular head to which a rope can be attached. These weight-bearing gadgets could be wedged into rock crevices as the mountaineers edged upward. Instead of pitons, these intrepid Sierra Nevada climbers used cheap ten-inch nails acquired at the local hardware store.

These avant-garde climbers were particularly intrigued by the Yosemite Valley's Lower and Higher Cathedral Spires—intimidating granite spikes that soar more than 2,000 feet above the valley floor. Throughout 1932 and 1933, many attempts were made, without the appropriate pitons, to climb both spires; all of the efforts failed, some just a few feet short of the top.

The climbers were strong, but their equipment was not. Frequently, the hardware store nails being used as ersatz pitons bent terrifyingly under the climbers' body weight. Three of the men—Richard Leonard, Jules Eichorn, and Bestor Robinson—realized the need for proper pitons and took on odd jobs to raise money to buy them. Eichorn earned a little extra cash by working for the famed photographer Ansel Adams, developing prints in the photographer's bathtub.

After securing the correct, high-tech pitons from the mail-order athletic equipment company SportHaus Schüster, in Munich, Germany, Leonard, Eichorn, and Robinson successfully climbed the Higher Cathedral Spire on April 15, 1934. The ascent took nine hours and used thirty-eight pitons. Once on the pinnacle, the trio raised an American flag, posed for a few congratulatory photographs, and then rapidly rappelled—using the Dülfersitz rappel technique, of course—down the spire to greet a crowd of delighted well-wishers far below. Their success paved the way for future mountain adventurers.

By 1956, the greatest challenges for Yosemite climbers were the unscaled faces of El Capitan and Half Dome. The gargantuan granite prow of El Cap reaches more than 3,500 feet above the Yosemite Valley floor, and the crest of the rounded knob of Half Dome soars 4,700 feet. Reconnaissance parties led by climbing legends Warren Harding, Royal Robbins, Jerry Gallwas, and Don Wilson scouted routes, and even made attempts, but the going was slow, frustrating, and ultimately unsuccessful.

By July 1957, this cadre of climbers believed the Northwest Face of Half Dome (a route covering 2,200 feet in elevation change) was ready to be scaled. Competing climbing teams ratcheted up their preparations. The eager Harding raced through the valley in his sporty Corvette intending to meet some colleagues to give it a go, but when he arrived he was disappointed to learn that Robbins, Gallwas, and Mike Sherrick had been on the face for four days already and were nearing the summit. The next day, the three men completed the dangerous climb. When they returned to the valley, the genial Harding greeted the men with hearty handshakes and much appreciated cold beer and sandwiches. This climb of the Northwest Face of Half Dome was the longest, most demanding, and most spine-tingling of all Yosemite rock climbs to date.

Harding was disappointed but he was also not one to give up easily, and he soon set his sights on conquering El Capitan. He and climbing companions Bill "Dolt" Feuerer and Mark Powell camped in El Capitan meadow and planned their route, fueled by copious consumption of cheap red wine. The course they chose was the central and longest part of the granite monument, covering 2,900 feet in elevation change.

Harding decided to use a "siege technique," a method frequently employed in Himalayan expeditions. In the "siege," teams of climbers establish miniature camps on ledges along the route, allowing them to stockpile provisions and make the ascent in phases. Harding and his team began the climb of El Capitan in July 1957.

Homemade equipment supplemented their more sophisticated gear. Most famously, the team used "stoveleg pitons"—four wooden pitons fabricated from the legs of a wood-burning stove. To cut costs, they used less-expensive hemp rope...until one line snapped and an unfortunate climber slid crazily down part of the rock face. From that point onward, Harding stated, "Cost be damned, from now on we are using nylon rope."

As word of their efforts spread, so many Yosemite Valley tourists gathered to gawk at Harding's crew that the National Park Service prohibited the climbers from working on their attempt during the summer tourist rush. Already they had been at work for months, and the Park Service, officially running out of patience, issued an ultimatum to Harding's team: finish the ascent by Thanksgiving or pull your ropes. In early November, Harding and the others made their final push. One hundred feet from the summit, the climbers encountered their most fearsome obstacle: a substantial granite overhang they called "the Nose." Their obstacle was formidable. Night was rapidly approaching. The fatigued but determined lead climber Harding pressed on, unaware that one of his dog-tired partners was drifting in and out of sleep. Inch by precious inch, they proceeded in darkness until the bruised but grateful climbers finally reached the summit of El Capitan at 6 a.m. on November 12, 1958—more than a year after beginning the endeavor and after forty-seven days of total climbing. On the summit, only minutes after the climbers had completed their ascent, a newspaper reporter (who had come up the "easy" way) asked the exhausted Harding how it felt to be the conqueror of El Capitan. He whispered this response: "Well, it seems to me that El Capitan is in a lot better shape than I am right now."

SIERRA SPOTLIGHT

Alex Honnold

Today, the mountaineering world is captivated by Alex Honnold, dubbed the "rock star of the climbing world" by the pun-happy *London Daily Mail*.

Honnold, born in Sacramento in 1985, is known for employing the "free solo" technique, which does not use ropes, although on some occasions he uses a method called "rope solo," in which a rope is used for safety purposes. This authentic Spider-man utilizes his exceptional agility and imposing upper-body strength to negotiate the rock towers of Yosemite and other daunting climbs around the world.

In 2008, Honnold free-soloed the Northwest Face of Half Dome in only two hours and fifty minutes, an effort that generally takes more traditional climbers about two days. On June 22, 2010, Honnold set a rope solo record on the Nose route of El Capitan at five hours and forty-nine minutes—the same route it had taken Warren Harding more than a year to climb. Honnold's record is even more remarkable when you consider that earlier the same day he had rope-soloed the Northwest Face of Half Dome in a little over two hours.

Yosemite Valley's El Capitan. In 2010, twenty-five-year-old phenom Alex Honnold climbed El Capitan in a little under six hours. Photograph attributed to Isaiah West Taber, c. 1870. From "California Views" [photograph album], Plate A 288, p. 8, from the California History Room Picture Collection: ** [Vault] f866 T14 (1880), No. 2009-1268, courtesy of the California State Library, Sacramento.

LIKE A ROLLERCOASTER, ONLY ROUGHER

The Tioga Pass Road

The Tioga Pass Road, leading to the eastern entrance of Yosemite National Park, is the eastern Sierra rollercoaster that some people refuse to ride. And it used to be much worse.

In 1915, energetic and persistent Stephen T. Mather became the assistant to the Secretary of the Interior and essentially created for himself the post of director of the brand new National Park Service. Mather felt that a top priority of the Park Service should be to increase public automobile access to the parks, and he was particularly interested in improving entry to Yosemite by 1915, as California was

The scary Tioga Pass Road, located in Lee Vining Canyon at the eastern entrance to Yosemite National Park. Photograph by Brian Grogan, 2001. From the series "Historic American Buildings Survey/Historic American Engineering Record/ Historic American Landscapes Survey," 2001, courtesy of the Library of Congress, Prints and Photographs Division, Washington, DC, HAER CAL,22-YOSEM,6—3.

to host two international expositions—in San Diego and San Francisco—that year.

Mather, a native Californian, remembered a road that many had forgotten—the Tioga Road (historically known as the Great Sierra Wagon Road), a privately owned, badly maintained, and barely passable horse and light-wagon toll road that bisected the park east to west and then dropped into the Great Basin. The route had not been widely used for years, the roadbed was in serious disrepair, its wooden bridges had rotted, and tolls had not been collected. According to Major H. C. Benson, acting superintendent of Yosemite National Park, the road in 1909 was in "wretched condition." The most intimidating section was the eastern fragment, which dipped nearly four thousand feet to Lee Vining, near Mono Lake, from the ten-thousand-foot-high Tioga Pass. This road was on the edge of the extremely steep Lee Vining Canyon, and the area was discouraged for use even as a foot trail. To this day, the official Yosemite Map and Visitors Guide strongly advises against hiking in the precipitous canyon.

In 1909, a rough, grueling state road had been constructed on this sheer eastern slope as far as Tioga Lake, and the Sierra Club urged the coupling of this new route with the old Tioga Road, "so as to afford one of the most wonderful trans-mountain roads in the world." But even this newly built road was treacherous. In 1912, Major W. T. Forsythe, acting superintendent of Yosemite, informed the Secretary of the Interior of the rescue of a wagon party on the road:

> Several wagons passed on the road last summer,...but also
> last summer I had to order a gratuitous issue of rations to
> a destitute family who were moving by wagon across the
> park from the east side by the Tioga Road because their
> team became exhausted on account of the difficult road and
> their food supply gave out before they could get through.

When Stephen Mather assumed the role as director of the National Park Service, he urged the government to purchase the Tioga Road, make the necessary repairs and improvements, and fully open the park to automobiles. He had already confirmed that the private owners were willing to sell the road for $15,000. Money aside, however, Mather was informed that the government appropriation process would take too long for the road to be available in 1915, and so he decided to take matters into his own hands. Mather told his assistant Horace Albright, "We've simply got to have that road. I'll buy the road myself and give it to the government."

Mather then ardently entered into the task of securing private donations for the purchase. If he could not raise the full $15,000, he pledged the remainder from his own considerable fortune. In the end, roughly half the purchase funds were contributed, Mather made up the difference, and California automobile clubs agreed to pay for the repairs.

As a public official, Mather could not legally convey the gift to the federal government, so the title was assigned to a young attorney named William E. Colby (who would later serve as president of the Sierra Club), who then donated the road. Legislation was required for Congress to accept the gift, so an act was introduced and passed and, in April 1915, the road was officially transferred to Yosemite National Park. An additional $30,000 was spent on road repairs.

On July 28, 1915, the Tioga Road was formally dedicated. Stephen Mather symbolically christened the project by breaking a bottle containing Pacific Ocean water on a rock dubbed the "$15,000 Rock," after the route's purchase price. In his 1954 book, *Steve Mather of the National Parks*, historian Robert Shankland describes the ceremonial automobile ride up the challenging twenty-one-mile Lee Vining–Tioga Pass grade by National Park Service officials and allies:

> Coming over the Lee Vining Road, they followed an interesting road…just a fraction more than one car wide with an unfenced drop-off as much as two thousand feet. Local men were at the wheels, and the one handling the open Studebaker that contained E. O. McCormick [vice president of the Southern Pacific Railroad], Emerson Hough [a prominent writer and naturalist], and Horace Albright [Mather's assistant] had not yet, though a native, become bored with the scenery. He would glance ahead briefly to gauge the curves, then rise from his seat, twist around, stare off over the grisly precipice into the distance, and with a hand he kept free for the purpose, point out the features of the landscape.

McCormick, up front, was mute with terror. In the rear, safe-side door open, Albright and Hough sat crouched to leap. Albright was trying to keep one hand on the open door and one foot on the running board and at the same time hold off Hough, who was clawing at him and hoarsely whispering over and over: "G-d d—n that scenery loving cuss, G-d d—n that scenery loving cuss!"

In the first year the road was open to automobile traffic, 350 cars made the trek, each one paying the five-dollar fee for the privilege of using the perilous pathway. One early traveler recalled his exhilarating climb to Tioga Pass:

These 21 miles are the most exasperating I have ever driven. I will personally guarantee there isn't a trickier road anywhere. It is a good deal like a roller coaster, only rougher! But if your car's in good shape, and you are confident of your driving skills; if you are looking for an adventurous route and breathtaking scenery, there's no better place to find it than along the Tioga Road.

Over the next half-century, this section of roadway was realigned, improved, and widened, but many motorists still trembled at the thought of driving the still narrow, twisting trail, skirting giant boulders and trees while on the edge of a cliff. Even as late as 1947, the American Automobile Association (AAA) warned: "It is not unusual to find people unused to mountain roads, who just go to pieces, freeze at the wheel and park their cars in the middle of the [Tioga Pass] road to wait for the Park Rangers or a kindly motorist to drive their cars the rest of the way." While there have been no fatalities reported on this stretch, there are numerous historical accounts of traffic jams due to troubles like overheating, vapor lock, fender benders, trailers stuck between trees and rocks, and other various and frequent mechanical problems. In 1961, the Tioga Road was regraded and the rolling roadway smoothed to create today's tamer route, featuring a number of turnouts and spectacular roadside vista points. Short portions of the original Tioga Pass Road remain for the daring, but most contemporary motorists stick to the present roadway, and some simply decline to traverse the Terrible Tioga at all, choosing to take a much longer, less nerve-jangling route.

SIERRA SPOTLIGHT

The Snowshed Highway

One of the most vexing problems for Sierra Nevada automobile traffic is the fabled "Sierra cement"—the impossibly deep, icy, and unyielding snowfall that blankets the range. Snow accumulation is difficult to clear under the best of circumstances, and in the early 1900s, the snow removal equipment was far from adequate for the task. Through the middle of the twentieth century, it was not uncommon for Sierra roadways to be closed for days, even weeks at a time when the prodigious snowbanks formed. In its December 1920 issue, *Popular Mechanics* offered a solution: as shown on the issue's cover, the magazine suggested

merging the Transcontinental Railroad line and the Lincoln Highway over Donner Summit. Their plan involved placing all-weather traffic lanes atop newly constructed, permanent train snow sheds. *Popular Mechanics* argued that maintenance would be easy and cheap, and it further opined that the costs of the cooperative construction efforts for the railroad and highway agencies would be minimal. The proposal did not receive serious consideration, but it was certainly an inventive, intriguing idea.

The December 1920 cover of *Popular Mechanics* magazine proposed a combination train snow shed and automobile highway over treacherous Donner Summit. From the California State Library General Collection Periodicals, Record #ca2550, Popular Mechanics Co., vol. 34, courtesy of the California State Library, Sacramento.

SELECTED
BIBLIOGRAPHY

Alta California. "Lo, the Poor Indian." April 17, 1855. Article on Indian kidnapping.

Arkelian, Marjorie Dakin. *Thomas Hill: The Grand View*. Oakland: Oakland Museum of California, 1980.

Baigell, Matthew. *Albert Bierstadt*. New York: Watson-Guptill, 1981.

Bancroft, Hubert Howe. *History of California*. San Francisco: A. L. Bancroft and Publishers, 1884–1890.

Beasley, Delilah L. *The Negro Trail Blazers of California*. Los Angeles, 1919. Reprint, San Francisco: R and E Research Associates, 1968.

Beesley, David. *Crow's Range: An Environmental History of the Sierra Nevada*. Reno: University of Nevada, 2004.

Bibby, Brian, and Dugan Aguilar. *Deeper than Gold: A Guide to Indian Life in the Sierra Foothills*. Berkeley: Heyday Books, 2004.

Book, Susan W. *The Chinese in Butte County, California, 1860–1920*. San Francisco: R and E Research Associates, 1976.

Bowles, Samuel. *Our New West: Records of Travel between the Mississippi River and the Pacific Ocean*. Hartford, CT: Hartford Publishing Co., 1869.

Brewer, William. *Up and Down California in 1860–1864*. New Haven, CT: Yale University Press, 1930.

Burge, Thomas L., Ward Eldredge, and William C. Tweed. "The Kaweah Colony: Utopia and Sequoia National Park." *Cultural Resource Management* 9 (2001). A publication of the National Park Service.

California Senate. *Chinese Immigration: Its Social, Moral, and Political Effect. Report of the Special Committee on Chinese Immigration to the California State Senate.* Sacramento, 1878, p. 236.

Chew, William. *Nameless Builders of the Transcontinental Railroad.* Bloomington, IN: Trafford, 2004.

Chico Butte Record. January 27, 1877. Article on "Supreme Order of the Caucasians."

Chinn, Thomas W., ed. *A History of the Chinese in California: A Syllabus.* San Francisco: Chinese Historical Society of America, 1969.

Chiu, Ping. *Chinese Labor in California, 1850–1880: An Economic Study.* Madison: State Historical Society of Wisconsin, 1967.

Chun-Chuen, Lai. Quoted in "Remarks of the Chinese Merchants of San Francisco, upon Governor Bigler's Message." *Oriental* (San Francisco). February 1, 1855.

Clark, W. B. *Gold Districts of California.* Bulletin 193. Sacramento: California Department of Conservation, Division of Mines and Geology, 1970.

Cook, Sherbourne F. *The Conflict between the California Indian and White Civilization.* Berkeley: University of California Press, 1976.

Coolidge, Mary Roberts. *Chinese Immigration.* New York: Henry Holt and Co., 1909.

Cox, Isaac. *Annals of Trinity County.* Eugene, OR: John Henry Nash of the University of Oregon, 1940.

Duncan, Jack E. *To Donner Pass from the Pacific.* Newcastle, CA: Jack E. Duncan, 2003.

Ehrgott, Alan. "History of the Wakamatsu Tea and Silk Colony." Coloma, CA: American River Conservancy, 2010.

Emerald Bay Route Studies. California Department of Public Works, Division of Highways, November 1960.

Farkas, Lani Ah Tye. *Bury My Bones in America: The Saga of a Chinese Family in California, 1852–1996.* Nevada City, CA: Carl Mautz Publishing, 1998.

Fradkin, Philip L. *The Seven States of California.* New York: Henry Holt, 1995.

Freeman, Christine. "Aaron Augustus Sargent: Nevada County's International Citizen." *Nevada County [California] Historical Society Bulletin*, vol. 32, no. 3 (July 1978): 13–21.

Gibson, Rev. Otis. *The Chinese in America.* Cincinnati: 1877.

Glasscock, C. B. *Lucky Baldwin: The Story of an Unconventional Success.* New York: A. L. Burt Company, 1933.

Goin, Peter. *Stopping Time: A Rephotographic Survey of Lake Tahoe.* Albuquerque: University of New Mexico Press, 1992.

Grass Valley Union. June 11, 1911. Article on the Tahoe Tavern Automobile Race.

Graydon, Charles K. *Trail of the First Wagons over the Sierra Nevada.* Tucson: Patrice Press, 1986.

Gronlund, Laurence. *The Co-operative Commonwealth in Its Outlines: An Exposition of Modern Socialism.* London: Swan Sonnenschein, 1896.

Hansen, Gladys, and William Heintz. *The Chinese in California.* San Francisco: Richard Abel and Company, 1970.

Hauser, Miska. *Selections from Hauser's Travel Book.* Washington, DC: Works Progress Administration, 1939.

Heizer, Robert F. *The Destruction of California Indians.* Lincoln: University of Nebraska Press, 1974.

Heizer, Robert F., and M. A. Whipple. *The California Indians: A Source Book.* Berkeley: University of California Press, 1951. Second edition, 1971.

Hittell, John S. *Yosemite: Its Wonders and Its Beauties.* Photographs by Eadweard Muybridge. San Francisco: H. H. Bancroft and Co., 1868.

Holland, S. Dennis. *Sierra Saints.* Placerville, CA: S. D. Holland Publishing, 1997.

Hsu, Madeline. *Dreaming of Gold, Dreaming of Home: Transnationalism and Migration between the United States and South China, 1882–1943.* Palo Alto: Stanford University Press, 2000.

Hutchings, James M. *In the Heart of the Sierras.* Oakland: Pacific Press Publishing, 1888.

_____. "The Mammoth Trees of California." *Hutchings' California Magazine*, vol. 3, no. 33 (March 1859).

James, George Wharton. *Lake of the Sky: Lake Tahoe.* Chicago: Charles T. Powner, 1956. Originally published in 1915.

James, Ronald M., and Susan A. James. *Castle in the Sky: George Whittell Jr. and the Thunderbird Lodge.* Lake Tahoe: Thunderbird Lodge Press, 2005.

Johnson, Paul C. *Sierra Album.* New York: Doubleday and Co., 1971.

Johnston-Dodds, Kimberly. "Early California Laws and Policies Related to California Indians." California Research Bureau, California State Library, CRB-02-014, September 2002.

Johnstone, Peter, ed. *Giants in the Earth: The California Redwoods.* Berkeley: Heyday, 2001.

Judah, Anna. "Letter to Hubert Howe Bancroft's History Company." December 14, 1889. Theodore Judah Papers, Bancroft Library, University of California, Berkeley.

Judah, Theodore. *A Practical Plan for Building the Pacific Railroad.* Written, San Francisco, January 1, 1857. Printed, Washington, DC: Henry Polkinhorn, 1857.

K'uang-min, Ch'en. *The Chinese in the Americas.* New York: 1950.

Kung, S. W. *Chinese in American Life: Some Aspects of Their History, Status, Problems, and Contributions.* Seattle: University of Washington, 1962.

Lesley, Lewis Burt, ed. *Uncle Sam's Camels: The Journal of May Humphreys Stacey, Supplemented by the Report of Edward Fitzgerald Beale, 1857–1858.* Cambridge, MA: Harvard University Press, 1929.

London Daily Mail. "'When You Are Climbing Well, The Fear Is Not There': Meet the Young Rock Star Hailed as the Best of His Generation." August 22, 2011. Article on Alex Honnold.

Loomis, Rev. A. W. "The Chinese Six Companies." *Overland Monthly* (September 1868): 221–227.

Lortie, Frank, et al. "The Folsom Powerhouse." California State Parks, Sacramento, 2012.

Mann, Ralph. *After the Gold Rush: Society in Grass Valley and Nevada City, California, 1849–1870.* Palo Alto: Stanford University Press, 1982.

Mansfield, George C. *History of Butte County, California, with Biographical Sketches.* Los Angeles: Historic Record, 1918.

Mark, Diane Mei Lin, and Ginger Chih. *A Place Called Chinese America.* Dubuque, IA: Kendall-Hart Publishing Co., 1982.

Mather, Stephen T. "Report of the Director of the National Park Service." *Reports of the Department of the Interior, 1919.* Two volumes. Washington, DC: Government Printing Office, 1920.

McGowan, Joseph A. *Sacramento: Heart of the Golden State.* Woodland Hills, CA: Windsor Publications, 1983.

McLaughlin, Mark. "Conquering Sierra Snow by Car." Tahoe Nugget #186. Mic-Mac Publishing. June 27, 2010. http://www.thestormking.com/tahoe_nuggets/Nugget_186/nugget_186.html

_____. "Conquering the Sierra by Car." *Northwoods Magazine* (May 2011): 5, 14.

Muir, John. "The Summer Flood of Tourists." *San Francisco Daily Evening Bulletin,* June 14, 1875.

Muir, John. "South Dome." *San Francisco Daily Evening Bulletin,* November 18, 1875.

_____. *Our National Parks.* Boston: Houghton, Mifflin and Co., 1901.

_____. "Letter to Howard Palmer, Secretary of the American Alpine Club." December 12, 1912.

_____. *The Mountains of California.* New York: Century, 1894. Reprint, 1913. *New York Times.* "Across the Sierra Nevada." July 12, 1868.

Muir, John, ed. *Picturesque California.* New York: J. Dewing Publishing, 1888.

Noy, Gary. "The Swan of Erin: The Enduring Legacy of Kate Hayes." *Grass Valley Union,* December 3, 2005, p. C1.

Noy, Gary, and Rick Heide, eds. *The Illuminated Landscape: A Sierra Nevada Anthology*. Berkeley: Heyday, 2010.

Ortiz, Bev. *It Will Live Forever: Traditional Yosemite Indian Acorn Preparation*. Berkeley: Heyday, 1991.

Pfaelzer, Jean. *Driven Out: The Forgotten War against Chinese Americans*. Berkeley: University of California Press, 2008.

Placer Herald. Jean Baptiste Charbonneau obituary. July 7, 1866.

Plumas National-Bulletin. "Death of Ah Tye." April 23, 1896.

Popular Mechanics. "Plan Road on Railroad Snowsheds." Vol. 34, no. 6 (December 1920). The cover of this issue was a full-color depiction of the snowshed highway.

Potts, Marie. *The Northern Maidu*. Happy Camp, CA: Naturegraph Publishers, 1977.

Proctor, A. Phimister. "An Ascent of Half Dome in 1884." *Sierra Club Bulletin*, vol. 31, no. 7 (1946): 1–9.

Quin, Richard H. "Tioga Road (HAER No. CA-149)." Historic American Engineering Record, National Park Service, 1991.

Ramsdell, H. J. "The Great Nevada Flume: A Perilous Ride." In *The Pacific Tourist: Adams and Bishop's Illustrated Trans-Continental Guide,* edited by Henry T. Williams, 219–224. New York: Adams and Bishop, 1881.

Ramsey, Alice Huyler. *Veil, Duster, and Tire Iron*. Pasadena, CA: Castle Press, 1961. Reprinted with additional material by Gregory Franzwa as *Alice's Drive: Republishing Veil, Duster and Tire Iron*. Tucson, AZ: Patrice Press, 2005.

Ramsey, Eleanor, and Janice S. Lewis. "History of Black Americans in California." In *Five Views: An Ethnic Historic Site Survey for California*. Sacramento: California Department of Parks and Recreation, Office of Historic Preservation, 1988.

Rawls, James J. *Indians of California: The Changing Image*. Norman: University of Oklahoma Press, 1984.

Richards, Gordon. "Echoes from the Past: The Stephens-Townsend-Murphy Party." *Sierra Sun* (Truckee, CA), September 24 and October 1, 2004.

Rourke, Constance. *Troupers of the Gold Coast, or the Rise of Lotta Crabtree*. New York: Harcourt, Brace and Co., 1928.

Sacramento Bee. "Grand Electrical Carnival." September 10, 1895.

Sacramento Union. "The Central Pacific Railroad." January 9, 1863.

Samuels, Peggy, Harold Samuels, Joan Samuels, and Daniel Fabian. *Techniques of the Artists of the American West*. Secaucus, NJ: Wellfleet Press, 1990.

San Francisco Call. "Son of President of Guatemala Sues for Damages from Being Thrown Downstairs while in Company of George Whittell Jr." January 7, 1908.

San Francisco Call. "Violins Wail But No Sob Is Heard." Vol. 105, no. 95 (March 5, 1909).

San Francisco Call. "Memorial for Ellen Clark Sargent." Vol. 110, no. 56 (July 26, 1911).

San Francisco Chronicle. "George B. Whittell Succumbs at 87." April 19, 1969.

San Francisco Daily Morning Call. "Up in El Dorado." January 1, 1870. Description of the Wakamatsu Tea and Silk Colony.

San Francisco Herald. December 14, 1856. Article on the case of the Indian girl Isabella.

San Francisco Newsletter. May 15, 1869. Article on Chinese workers placing the final ties of the Central Pacific Railroad.

San Francisco Whig. "Lola Montez." June 3, 1853.

Sandmeyer, Elmer Clarence. *The Anti-Chinese Movement in California.* Urbana: University of Illinois Press, 1939.

Saxton, Alexander. "The Army of Canton in the High Sierra." *Pacific Historical Review* 35 (1966): 141–152.

Schallenberger, Moses. *The Opening of the California Trail: The Story of the Stevens Party from the Reminiscences of Moses Schallenberger as set down for H. H. Bancroft about 1885.* Schallenberger's account was originally recorded by Mary Sheldon Barnes and first published in *Pen Pictures from the Garden of the World,* edited by Horace S. Foote. Chicago: The Lewis Publishing Company, 1888. Reprinted with additional material as *The Opening of the California Trail,* George R. Stewart, ed. Berkeley: University of California Press, 1953.

Scott, Amy, ed. *Yosemite: Art of an American Icon.* Berkeley: University of California Press, 2006.

Seymour, Bruce. *Lola Montez: A Life.* New Haven: Yale University Press, 1996.

Shankland, Robert. *Steve Mather of the National Parks.* New York: Alfred A. Knopf, 1954.

Shields, Scott A. *Artists at Continent's End: The Monterey Peninsula Art Colony, 1875–1907.* Berkeley: University of California Press, 2006.

Sierra Nevada Ecosystem Report: Final Report to Congress (SNEP). Wildlands Resources Center Report No. 37. Davis, CA: Centers for Water and Wildland Resources, 1996.

Southern Pacific Railroad Company. "California for the Tourist." Promotional pamphlet. San Francisco: Sunset Publishing House, 1912.

Standing Guard: Telling Our Stories. Rocklin, CA: Sierra College Press, 2002.

Stanford, Leland. *Statement Made to the President of the United States and the Secretary of the Interior on the Progress of the Work, October 10th, 1865,* pp. 7–8. Sacramento: H. S. Crocker and Co., 1865.

Stewart, George R. *The California Trail.* New York: McGraw-Hill, 1962.

_____. "History of the Kaweah Colony." Unpublished manuscript housed in the Tulare County Library. Based on a newspaper article in the *Visalia Delta,* December 3, 1891, p. 3.

Stewart, William Morris. *Reminiscences of Senator William M. Stewart of Nevada.* New York: Neale Publishing Co., 1908.

Strong, Douglas H. *Tahoe: An Environmental History.* Lincoln: University of Nebraska, 1984.

Takaki, Ronald. *Strangers from a Different Shore: A History of Asian Americans.* Boston: Little, Brown and Co., 1989.

Thompson and West. *History of Nevada County.* Oakland: Thompson and West, 1880.

_____. *History of Placer County.* Oakland: Thompson and West, 1882.

Thunderbird Lodge Preservation Society. http://www.thunderbirdtahoe.org.

Trexler, Keith A. *The Tioga Road, 1883–1961.* El Portal, CA: Yosemite Association, 1961. Revised in 1975 and 1980.

Tung, William. *The Chinese in America.* Dobbs Ferry, NY: Oceana Publications, 1974.

Twain, Mark. *Roughing It.* Hartford, CT: American Publishing Company, 1872. Reprint, New York: Harper and Brothers, 1906.

Tyler, Daniel. *A Concise History of the Mormon Battalion in the Mexican War, 1846–1847.* Chicago: Rio Grande Press, 1964. Originally published in 1881.

United States Bureau of the Census. Documents 1850–1910.

United States Department of the Interior, National Park Service. "Whittell Estate." National Register of Historic Places Nomination, No. #00001207, October 27, 2000.

Vischer, Edward. *Vischer's Views of California—#12, The Mammoth Grove Hotel, Grounds and General View of the Forest [Calaveras Big Trees, California].* Edward Visher Publisher, c. 1862.

Walsh, Basil. *Catherine Hayes: The Hibernian Prima Donna.* Dublin: Irish Academic Press, 2000.

Wells, Harry L. "Gold Lake." *Overland Monthly,* November 1884.

Werner, Emmy. *Pioneer Children of the Journey West.* Boulder, CO: Westview Press, 1995.

Wey, Nancy. "Chinese Americans in California." In *Five Views: An Ethnic History for California.* Sacramento: California Department of Parks and Recreation, Office of Historic Preservation, 1988.

Wheat, Carl I. "A Sketch of the Life of Theodore D. Judah." *California Historical Society Quarterly,* vol. 4, no. 3 (September 1925): 219–271. This article features a letter written by Anna Judah in 1889 that was originally published in the journal *Themis* on December 14, 1889. The original, unedited letter is in the collection of The Bancroft Library, University of California, Berkeley.

Withington, Carol. *The Black Pioneers of Yuba County*. Yuba City: Sir Speedy Printing, 1987.

Wolfe, Linnie Marsh, ed. *John of the Mountains: The Unpublished Journals of John Muir.* Madison: University of Wisconsin Press, 1979.

Yan, Geling. Quoted in the transcript of "Becoming American: The Chinese Experience," Program One, p. 5. Produced by PBS, 2003.

Yung, Judy. *Unbound Feet: A Social History of Chinese Women in San Francisco*. Berkeley: University of California Press, 1995.

Zo, Kil Young. *Chinese Emigrants to the United States, 1850–1880*. New York: Arno Press, 1978.

ACKNOWLEDGMENTS

The journey for *Sierra Stories: Tales of Dreamers, Schemers, Bigots, and Rogues* has been long. Lifelong, in fact. I owe my fascination with Sierra Nevada history and culture, and my appreciation for the beauty and value of the regional landscape, to my parents, Howard and Velma Noy. They sparked my interest in the Range of Light very early in life, perhaps in utero. As have many, my parents came from elsewhere to live in the Sierra Nevada—my mom as part of the Dust Bowl migration from Oklahoma, and my dad as a member of a Cornish gold mining family from Montana. They settled, met, and married in Grass Valley, my Nevada County birthplace and hometown. My earliest memories are of traveling with my mom and dad throughout our home territory, seeing and sharing in their delight in every fresh discovery, every wonderful adventure. My parents inspired my love of the Sierra, and *Sierra Stories* is dedicated to them.

My deepest thanks to my friend and guru, Malcolm Margolin, the publisher of Heyday, for his wise advice, constant encouragement, and for his lovely and thoughtful introduction to *Sierra Stories*. Much-deserved praise also goes to editors Gayle Wattawa and Lisa K. Marietta, outreach director Lillian Fleer, designers Ashley Ingram and Jami Spittler, art director Diane Lee, and all the extraordinary staff of Heyday. Along the trail, they have become cherished friends and colleagues.

My thanks and appreciation go to my Sierra College Press family, with whom I have traveled many miles and experienced much joy and achievement. I am especially grateful to editor in chief Joe Medeiros and my *Illuminated Landscape* coeditor, Rick Heide, for many pleasurable hours in their company and for their boundless support; your friendship means more than I could ever adequately express.

Extra-special kudos is extended to Gabriel Schlaefer, who was responsible for securing the image permissions for *Sierra Stories*. Thanks, Gabe, for your hard work, commitment, and professionalism.

And, finally, I would be wholly remiss if I did not acknowledge the people who made this book possible: the endlessly captivating, constantly surprising characters of the Range of Light.

ABOUT THE AUTHOR

Photo by Mike Price. Courtesy of Sierra College Press.

A Sierra Nevada native, Gary Noy has taught history at Sierra Community College in Rocklin, California, since 1987. A graduate of UC Berkeley and CSU Sacramento, he is the founder and former director of the Sierra College Center for Sierra Nevada Studies and the editor in chief emeritus of Sierra College Press. In 2006, the Oregon-California Trails Association (OCTA), a national historical society, selected Noy as Educator of the Year. He is the author of *Distant Horizon: Documents from the Nineteenth-Century American West* (1999) and the coeditor, with Rick Heide, of *The Illuminated Landscape: A Sierra Nevada Anthology* (2010).

SIERRA COLLEGE PRESS

In 2002, Sierra College Press was formed to publish *Standing Guard: Telling Our Stories* as part of the Standing Guard Project's examination of Japanese American internment during World War II. Since then Sierra College Press has grown into the first complete academic press operated by a community college in the United States.

The mission of Sierra College Press is to inform and inspire scholars, students, and general readers by disseminating ideas, knowledge, and academic scholarship of value concerning the Sierra Nevada region. Sierra College Press endeavors to reach beyond the library, laboratory, and classroom to promote and examine this unique geography. For more information, please visit www.sierracollege.edu/press.

EDITOR IN CHIEF: Joe Medeiros

BOARD OF DIRECTORS: Rebecca Bocchicchio, Keely Carroll, Kerrie Cassidy, Mandy Davies, Daniel DeFoe, Dave Ferrari, Tom Fillebrown, Rebecca Gregg, Brian Haley, Robert Hanna, Rick Heide, Jay Hester, David Kuchera, Carol Hoge, Roger Lokey, Lynn Medeiros, Sue Michaels, Gary Noy, Mike Price, Jennifer Skillen, Barbara Vineyard

ADVISORY BOARD: Terry Beers, David Beesley, Charles Dailey, Frank DeCourten, Patrick Ettinger, Tom Killion, Tom Knudson, Gary Kurutz, Scott Lankford, John Muir Laws, Beverly Lewis, Malcolm Margolin, Mark McLaughlin, Bruce Pierini, Kim Stanley Robinson, jesikah maria ross, Michael Sanford, Lee Stetson, Catherine Stifter, Rene Yung

Special thanks to Sierra College Friends of the Library, a major financial supporter.

HEYDAY
into California

ABOUT HEYDAY

Heyday is an independent, nonprofit publisher and unique cultural institution. We promote widespread awareness and celebration of California's many cultures, landscapes, and boundary-breaking ideas. Through our well-crafted books, public events, and innovative outreach programs we are building a vibrant community of readers, writers, and thinkers.

THANK YOU

It takes the collective effort of many to create a thriving literary culture. We are thankful to all the thoughtful people we have the privilege to engage with. Cheers to our writers, artists, editors, storytellers, designers, printers, bookstores, critics, cultural organizations, readers, and book lovers everywhere!

We are especially grateful for the generous funding we've received for our publications and programs during the past year from foundations and hundreds of individual donors. Major supporters include:

Anonymous (5); Alliance for California Traditional Arts; Arkay Foundation; Judy Avery; James J. Baechle; Paul Bancroft III; Richard and Rickie Ann Baum; BayTree Fund; S. D. Bechtel, Jr. Foundation; Jean and Fred Berensmeier; Berkeley Civic Arts Program and Civic Arts Commission; Joan Berman; John Briscoe; Lewis and Sheana Butler; California Civil Liberties Public Education Program; Cal Humanities; California Indian Heritage Center Foundation; California State Parks Foundation; Keith Campbell Foundation; Candelaria Fund; John and Nancy Cassidy Family Foundation, through Silicon Valley Community Foundation; Charles Edwin Chase; Graham Chisholm; The Christensen Fund; Jon Christensen; Community Futures Collective; Compton Foundation; Creative Work Fund; Lawrence Crooks; Nik Dehejia; Frances Dinkelspiel and Gary Wayne; The Durfee Foundation; Earth Island Institute; The Fred Gellert

Family Foundation; Fulfillco; The Wallace Alexander Gerbode Foundation; Nicola W. Gordon; Wanda Lee Graves and Stephen Duscha; David Guy; The Walter and Elise Haas Fund; Coke and James Hallowell; Steve Hearst; Cindy Heitzman; Historic Resources Group; Sandra and Charles Hobson; Donna Ewald Huggins; Humboldt Area Foundation; JiJi Foundation; The James Irvine Foundation; Claudia Jurmain; Marty and Pamela Krasney; Robert and Karen Kustel; Guy Lampard and Suzanne Badenhoop; Christine Leefeldt, in celebration of Ernest Callenbach and Malcolm Margolin's friendship; Thomas Lockard; Thomas J. Long Foundation; Judith and Brad Lowry-Croul; Michael McCone; Nion McEvoy and Leslie Berriman; Giles W. and Elise G. Mead Foundation; Michael Mitrani; Moore Family Foundation; The MSB Charitable Fund; Richard Nagler; National Endowment for the Arts; National Wildlife Federation; Native Cultures Fund; The Nature Conservancy; Nightingale Family Foundation; Northern California Water Association; Ohlone-Costanoan Esselen Nation; The David and Lucile Packard Foundation; Panta Rhea Foundation; David Plant; Alan Rosenus; The San Francisco Foundation; Greg Sarris; William Somerville; Martha Stanley; Radha Stern, in honor of Malcolm Margolin and Diane Lee; Roselyne Chroman Swig; Swinerton Family Fund; Sedge Thomson and Sylvia Brownrigg; TomKat Charitable Trust; Michael and Shirley Traynor; The Roger J. and Madeleine Traynor Foundation; Lisa Van Cleef and Mark Gunson; Patricia Wakida; John Wiley & Sons, Inc.; Peter Booth Wiley and Valerie Barth; Bobby Winston; Dean Witter Foundation; The Work-in-Progress Fund of Tides Foundation; and Yocha Dehe Wintun Nation.

BOARD OF DIRECTORS

GETTING INVOLVED

To learn more about our publications, events, membership club, and other ways you can participate, please visit www.heydaybooks.com.